The Home–School Connection

Lessons Learned in a Culturally and Linguistically Diverse Community

Flora V. Rodríguez-Brown

Routledge
Taylor & Francis Group

NEW YORK AND LONDON

First published 2009
by Routledge
270 Madison Ave, New York, NY 10016

Simultaneously published in the UK
by Routledge
2 Park Square, Milton Park, Abingdon, Oxon OX14 4RN

Routledge is an imprint of the Taylor & Francis Group, an informa business

© 2009 Taylor & Francis

Typeset in Sabon by Wearset Ltd, Boldon, Tyne and Wear
Printed and bound in the United States of America on
acid-free paper by Walsworth Publishing Company, Marceline, MO

Library of Congress Cataloging in Publication Data
Rodríguez-Brown, Flora V.
The home–school connection: Lessons learned in a culturally
and linguistically diverse community/Flora V. Rodríguez-
Brown.
p. cm.
Includes bibliographical references.
1. Home and school–Illinois. 2. Family literacy
programs–Illinois. 3. Project FLAME I. Title.
LC225.32.I44R63 2008
371.19'2–dc22
2007050917

ISBN 10: 0-8058-5784-2 (hbk) 140.00
ISBN 10: 0-8058-5785-0 (pbk) 43.95
ISBN 10: 1-4106-1770-X (ebk) 43.95

ISBN 13: 978-0-8058-5784-9 (hbk)
ISBN 13: 978-0-8058-5785-6 (pbk)
ISBN 13: 978-1-4106-1770-5 (ebk)

The Home–School Connection

In this book the home–school connection is viewed as a two-way road where parents and teachers learn from each other, in order to make learning relevant to children. Family literacy is presented as parent involvement within a "learning at home" perspective. *The Home–School Connection* provides information and support to those working with culturally and linguistically diverse families.

The Project FLAME program used as context for this book is a comprehensive family literacy model supported by a strong sociocultural framework, based on current research on cultural ways of learning and theories of multiliteracies and discourse. The model highlights the relevance of parents' knowledge, cultural ways, and discourses in sharing literacy knowledge with their children.

Demographic data confirm the steadily increasing numbers of culturally and linguistically diverse students in U.S. public schools today. A pressing need exists for models and programs that effectively serve the educational needs of this population. Addressing issues related to development, implementation, and effectiveness of a program model that fulfills this need, this book is an essential resource for educators, community workers, and researchers interested in the relevance of the home–school connection in relation to children's school success.

Flora V. Rodríguez-Brown is a Professor in Curriculum and Instruction, and in the Literacy, Language and Culture Program at the University of Illinois at Chicago.

Contents

Tables

Preface

Originally, like many other people, I thought of the home–school connection as being unidirectional, that is, parents supporting their children's learning at home as a way to help them do well in school. It was not until I considered the irrelevance of many school activities to the lives of children who are culturally and linguistically diverse that I started thinking about issues of discontinuity between home and school. Then, I realized that teachers also have a role in home–school connections. With that understanding, I began to visualize the home–school connection as a two-way street where both parents and teachers contribute to the creation of a bridge that supports children's transitions between home and school. This book is about how I arrived at that conclusion.

It was 1989 when I first decided that I wanted to get involved in family literacy with a Latino community in Chicago. At the time, I was not aware of the amount of literacy that exists in Latino households. I had read government surveys that showed that there are not many books in Latino homes and that parents are not involved in their children's education. As an academic, I worked with Timothy Shanahan to design a family literacy program model, Project FLAME (Rodríguez-Brown & Shanahan, 1989), which was funded by the United States Department of Education for six years. Eventually, it became an Academic Excellence model and was disseminated nationally for five years. The program was based on what we thought was relevant for parents to learn about early literacy and on the importance of parents' involvement in their children's literacy learning at home. We never thought about whether there was any literacy learning already occurring in the home, or the fact that the parents we planned to work with were culturally different and might have different views about their role as teachers. As I have written elsewhere (Rodríguez-Brown, 2001a, 2004), our program was a "functional" family literacy program, which fulfilled the requirements of the funding agency. However, in many ways, it was decontextualized from the community where it was to be implemented. It was a top-down model. Eventually, I realized that for the program to be successful and lasting, we had to allow some input and sense of ownership from the participants. It was necessary for the program to become "critical" to the needs of the community we were serving.

Although the literacy curriculum design for the program has been maintained, we have since allowed parents to add their voices to the planning of specific activities for different family literacy sessions that are offered through the program. We believe the program has to be relevant to the parents for it to make a difference in their lives, in the ways they deal with literacy learning at home, and in how they make connections with schools and teachers.

Currently, FLAME is implemented in four demonstration sites serving 12 schools in Chicago. It is now funded through donations from foundations and corporations. The program model has been adopted in more than 50 sites nationwide. Although the literacy components of FLAME have not changed, the program has been successful for many years due to the sociocultural framework that supports the work with parents who are linguistically and culturally diverse. We also are aware of the need for parents and communities of every culture to take some ownership of the program, so we try to adapt program activities to the needs of the specific areas where we work.

My thinking about the field of family literacy has evolved through the years. I have learned more about theory, research, and practice in regards to parental involvement. Following Joyce Epstein's (1995) typology, I view family literacy as one type of parental involvement that includes literacy learning at home. For this reason I frame the contents of this book in relation to parental involvement and family literacy.

Overview

Part I of this book focuses on the broader issues of parental involvement and family literacy as one type of parental involvement. Chapter 1 describes the role of parental involvement in school achievement. Then it discusses theory, policy, research, and practice in relation to different views of parental involvement. Chapter 2 deals with various definitions and perspectives of the term family literacy. It also discusses theory, policy, research, and practice in the area of family literacy.

Part II comprises four chapters that describe my work in family literacy in the Latino community in Chicago. Chapter 3 explains the Project FLAME model of family literacy, including changes that have occurred since it was originally designed. Chapter 4 reviews sociocultural research and theories that support the development of a theoretical sociocultural framework for work with culturally and linguistically different families. This framework has allowed us to develop a set of principles for everyday work with participants in the program.

Chapter 5 examines the effectiveness of the FLAME program through an analysis of data that has been collected through the years. The results show how the program affects participant parents and, indirectly, their children. Qualitative data is also used to provide examples of changes within specific families who have been involved in the program. This chapter includes a section in which parents write about how Project FLAME has made a difference in their home literacy lives.

Chapter 6 is a recollection of lessons learned about program development, implementation, and evaluation. It relates what has been learned through working with families and the present understanding of what is needed to make family literacy programs successful.

In Part III, the focus is on teachers and their role in establishing and maintaining effective home–school connections. Chapter 7 deals with the school-to-home connection. The work of Norma Gonzalez and Luis Moll is highlighted as it describes the training of teachers as ethnographers who then learn about knowledge and resources that exist in their school communities. More important to this endeavor are the examples from teachers who participated in the "Funds of Knowledge" project. They explain how they have integrated their new knowledge into their school curriculum. The chapter also explores ways in which out-of-school programs contribute to the home–school connection.

Chapter 8 describes specific ways in which teachers have incorporated out-of-school knowledge into the curriculum to support children's literacy learning at school. It highlights a teacher's efforts to learn whether and how parents whose children are bused to a community school support their children's homework. Two action research projects show how these teachers were successful in creating meaningful school-to-home connections in their classrooms. Both projects were linked to state learning standards.

Chapter 9 describes my efforts to make teachers aware of the importance of the school-to-home connection by offering a university class with this focus. Through the description of individual projects carried out in their classrooms, two teachers show how they applied what they learned in a college class about the relevance of bringing out-of-school knowledge into their school curriculum. These projects used community and/or home knowledge as resources to enhance the connection between home and school and make the curriculum more relevant for children in the classrooms.

Finally, in the Epilogue, I revisit lessons learned. I also iterate the home–school connection as a two-way street whereby teachers and parents make contributions to congruency in learning and continuity between home and school that can enhance the opportunities for school success for all children, but particularly for those who are culturally and linguistically diverse.

Acknowledgments

I would like to take this opportunity to thank all the FLAME parents from whom I have learned so much through the years. This book would not be a reality without their effort, caring, and sharing of knowledge while creating opportunities for their children's learning and at the same time using their own cultural ways and discourses. Gracias por su interés y esfuerzo para crear un mundo mejor para sus niños.

Through the years, we have shared our activities with a very talented, caring, and energetic group of teaching assistants from the University of Illinois at Chicago. They have contributed to making our work with the parents a real sharing and learning experience. Thank you for understanding and respecting the parents' contributions to our program and the relevance of their knowledge to the success of Project FLAME.

In writing this book, I have been blessed with the help of two gifted editors, Dr. Sandra Gandy and Ms. Elizabeth Greiner, who helped me make this text more readable and interesting. I would like to thank Naomi Silverman and Kelly Alderson for their support and patience during this endeavor. I also want to thank the reviewers for their comments and recommendations in order to make this a better publication.

Finally, I would like to thank my family, my husband James M., sons James A. and John A., daughter-in-law, Nikki, and my grandchildren James Roth and Bailey Madison Brown for bringing so much joy into my life and being patient while I was writing. You are a great bunch! This book is dedicated to all of you.

Flora V. Rodríguez-Brown

Part I

Parental Involvement and Family Literacy

Part I explains parental involvement and family literacy in order to lay a foundation for the later discussion of the home–school connection. The work of Joyce Epstein (1995) is central to any exploration of parental involvement. Epstein explains that the view taken by educators can determine the ways in which parents get involved with their children's learning and with the schools. If teachers and school staff think of children as only students, they will also think of the family as a separate unit that is not involved in the education of the students. However, if they think of the students as children, they will more often consider both the family and the community to be potential contributors to the children's education.

Chapter 1 begins with a definition of parental involvement and a look at research on the effectiveness of parental involvement and social and cultural differences. It also examines federal, state, and local policy regarding the obligations of school districts to provide programs that foster parental involvement. Finally, organizations that provide resources for developing and implementing a program of parental involvement are mentioned.

Chapter 2 defines family literacy as one kind of parental involvement and as literacy learning that occurs at home in culturally relevant ways that already exist in culturally and linguistically diverse families. McCarthey (1997) states that "access to literacy has been socially and culturally channeled, favoring the white, middle-class ways of making meaning at the expense of others" (p. 146). For students who are not members of the middle class, learning at school might be more difficult:

> Although virtually all children in a literate society have numerous experiences with print before coming to school, race, social class and cultural and linguistic background play a role in children's sense-making of those literacy practices.
>
> (McCarthey, 1997, p. 146)

These views are shared by many other researchers and are central to the discussion of family literacy. Chapter 2 also describes programs identified as family literacy.

Chapter I

Parental Involvement
Research, Policy, and Resources

Introduction

The home–school connection discussed in this book is two-way in that schools and teachers support parents with information and ideas about how to work with their children at home, while teachers become knowledgeable about parents' cultural ways of learning, their knowledge, and aspirations for their children. As a result, teachers learn to see parents as resources in their homes, classrooms, and schools; and parents can work in partnership with the community and/or school personnel with the goal of enhancing the academic achievement of all children. In fact, effective education requires that schools and families work together and form partnerships where parents and teachers learn to respect and trust each other and to collaborate in the planning, development, and implementation of activities that support children's learning both at home and at school.

Personal commitments and abilities might limit some parents' involvement in school activities, but at home, all parents can provide some level of academic support to their children. Learning at home, one component of Epstein's (1995) typology of parental involvement, is the focus of this book. It specifically discusses ways that parents can support literacy learning as their children prepare to enter school as well as during their school years. Literacy, because it is social in nature, is an area of the school curriculum in which parents can have more of an impact on learning, particularly at home. Before dealing with issues of family literacy and sociocultural practices involved in literacy learning, it is important to look at the larger picture of parental involvement. This chapter begins with a definition and then discusses the impact of parental involvement on learning, barriers to involvement, and current policy and practices for parental involvement.

Defining Parental Involvement

Parental involvement has many different meanings, depending on the context in which it is used. In general, the term is used to describe different forms of parental participation in their children's education and with the schools. Researchers, policy makers, and teachers should be aware of the multiple meanings of the term so they can use the definition that best fits their context.

Attempts to define parental involvement have been influenced mostly by the work of Joyce Epstein, who has been researching this area for many years (1984a, 1984b, 1987, 1991, 1995). In the past, parental involvement in schools usually meant attending Parent-Teacher Association (PTA) meetings and parent-teacher conferences. Some parents might help organize fundraising activities or serve as chaperones for field trips. However, Epstein (1995) expands the concept and identifies six types of parental involvement in schools: parenting, communicating, volunteering, learning at home, decision making, and collaborating with the community. These categories are derived from Epstein's research findings and are related to her model of spheres of influence, which deals with the overlap among schools, families, and communities. Epstein's typology has been adopted by the National PTA (2003) as National Standards for Parental Involvement. These standards have been endorsed by more than 30 national and educational parental involvement organizations (see PTA Standards Handbook at www.pta.org).

According to Epstein, the various types of parental involvement provide parents with different opportunities to participate in their children's schools through activities that are consistent with their own comfort level and availability, while still contributing to their children's education. For example, some parents support their children by attending school functions, parent–teacher conferences, or other activities in the school, and by being responsive to schools. Parents also become involved in their children's learning when they model behaviors such as reading and writing, monitor homework, interact with their children, and provide opportunities for learning at home and in the community. Parental involvement can include the role of volunteers and advocates in the school, as well as participation in school governance and decision making related to the development and planning of school activities and programs. Epstein finds that the greatest impact on student achievement comes from family participation in well-designed, at-home activities. This impact is effective across different families' racial background and/or parents' formal education.

Other researchers have investigated parental involvement and identified different components (Flaxman & Inger, 1992; Hester, 1989; Moore, 1991; Weisz, 1990). Weisz restricted his suggestions to roles that parents might assume as volunteers in school. Hester (1989) emphasized the importance of communication and identified four components for parental involvement: parents as teachers, parents as supporters of school activities, parents as learners, and parents as advocates. In 1993, The National PTA Board of Directors endorsed three types of parental involvement as follows: parents as the first educators in the home, parents as partners in the school, and parents as advocates for all children and youth in society.

More recently, Jones (2001) saw a need to redefine parental involvement. She felt that what schools have traditionally called parental involvement does not necessarily influence student achievement. Although classroom activities such as volunteering might be ideal for some parents, those with daytime jobs or young children at home are usually not available during school hours. Jones stated that parents who volunteer should participate in activities such as tutoring in support of children's achievement. This type of involvement requires planning, should include many families, and needs to be ongoing.

For the purposes of this book, Epstein's (1995) typology of parental involvement is used with the focus on learning at home.

Research

A look at research involving parental involvement can provide answers to questions such as the following: What does research tell us about the influence of parental involvement on student achievement? Why is parental involvement relevant to schools and communities? Is parental involvement a way to support children's interest in schooling and a way to increase student achievement, or is it just an added responsibility for teachers and schools?

There are literally hundreds of documents on the subject of parental involvement including research reports, books, journal articles, expert opinions, theory papers, position statements, program descriptions, and guidelines for setting up programs. The types of parental involvement investigated include telephone and written home–school communications, attendance at school functions, parents serving as classroom volunteers, parent-teacher conferences, homework assistance/tutoring, home educational enrichment, and parental involvement in decision making and other aspects of school governance. Researchers focused on a variety of student outcome areas, including general achievement; achievement in reading, math, or other specific curricular areas; and an array of attitudinal and behavioral outcomes.

Parental Involvement and School Achievement

Henderson (1987) reviewed 66 studies conducted in the area of school achievement and parental involvement. She found that when parents are involved in their children's learning at home, children do better in school. Also, when parents are involved at school, their children go further in school, and the schools the children attend are better. In a meta-analysis of 2,500 studies, Walberg (1984) found that an academically supportive home environment is one of the first determinants of learning outcomes. The effect of what he calls "curriculum at home" (home learning activities that support school learning) is twice as large as family socioeconomic status.

Reynolds, Temple, Robertson, and Mann (2001) reported that parents' expectations of their child's educational attainment and satisfaction with the child's education at school are the most consistent predictors of children's academic achievement. Also, in a longitudinal study of the effects of parental involvement on elementary students' achievement, Epstein (1984b) found significant increases over time, particularly in reading skills. Desimone (1999), using data from a longitudinal study done in 1988, found significant and meaningful differences between student achievement and parental involvement according to students' race, ethnicity, and family income. This contrasts with Epstein's (1995) earlier findings of no differences across race, ethnicity, and income.

Olmstead and Rubin (1983) evaluated the effectiveness of the Follow Through Program, one of the first U.S. government funded programs that supported learning at home. The program was based on home visits where paraprofessionals showed parents how to teach their children at home. Some of the behaviors taught in the training included: (a) explain to the learner what you are going to do; (b) give the learner time to become familiar with the materials; (c) ask questions that have more than one correct answer; and (d) entice the learner to ask questions and let the learner know when his/her answers are wrong. The researchers examined the relationship between parent behaviors taught in the program and their children's achievement. They found changes in parental behaviors that positively affected children's achievement. They also found a difference in parents' behaviors between those who participated in the program and those in a control group.

More recent syntheses or reviews of literature related to parental involvement also have explored the relationship between parental involvement and school achievement (Baker & Soden, 1997; Boethel, 2003; Henderson & Mapp, 2002; Jeynes, 2003; Mattingly, Prislin, McKenzie, Rodríguez, & Kayzar, 2002). All of these synthesis studies regard the relationship between parental involvement and achievement as encouraging, but state that there is still a need for further confirmation of this issue because of conflicting results. However, some of these studies warrant a closer look.

Baker and Soden (1997) reviewed 200 studies published between 1970 and 1996. Of these studies, 108 were related to relationships between parental involvement and children's achievement, but only three used experimental designs. The results of these three studies showed some evidence of a positive impact of parental involvement on student achievement.

In their synthesis of research on parental involvement, Henderson and Mapp (2002) examined 51 studies published between 1995 and 2002. Following their analysis, the authors concluded that:

> Taken as a whole, these studies found a positive ... relationship between family involvement and benefits for students, including improved academic achievement. This relationship holds across families of all economic, racial/ethnic, and educational backgrounds and for students at all ages.
>
> (p. 24)

Mattingly et al. (2002) selected 41 studies for their synthesis. Only four experimental studies met their criteria. Of those four studies, only two, done in the 1970s, showed an increase in achievement among children whose parents participated in an intervention program. This is another example of conflicting results.

Parental involvement in minority families was discussed by Jeynes (2003) in a meta-analysis of 20 studies that involved African American, Latino, and Asian American families at different income levels. Looking at the relationship between parental involvement and school achievement of children from those families, Jeynes found some variations across populations but concluded that parental involvement had a significant impact on the achievement of the minority children included in the studies.

Another study that looked at the achievement of Mexican American children found similar results. In a longitudinal study, Keith and Lichtman (1994) reported a significant influence of parental involvement on the achievement of Mexican American children.

Finally, a synthesis by Boethel (2003) included 64 studies that examined issues of diversity in relation to student achievement and family, community, and school connections. The synthesis discussed the role of minority and/or low-income families in supporting their children's school achievement. It also addressed barriers to parental involvement for minority and low-income families. The synthesis produced these seven main findings, which are summarized below:

1   In spite of the fact that all families have high aspirations for their children, there is limited research that shows a relationship between parental high aspirations and student achievement.
2   Minority families are actively involved in their children's schooling, although their involvement might be different from that of white, middle-class families.
3   Reports from schools and families about parental involvement are inconsistent.
4   Research studies have identified barriers for minority families to becoming involved with their children's schooling. These barriers include contextual constraints, language differences, cultural beliefs, and lack of knowledge, among others.
5   There are limited and inconsistent research findings as to whether an increase in parental involvement leads to improved academic achievement.
6   Some intervention strategies show promise in enhancing parental involvement, but there is not much research available in this area.
7   According to some studies, it is necessary to address the complexity of interactions between family, community, and schools as a way to close the achievement gap among minority and low-income populations.

The purpose for describing the results of different research syntheses on parental involvement, using a variety of selection criteria for the data involved in the analysis, is to allow common findings to surface. Although results of studies are sometimes contradictory, the general tendency is toward a positive relationship between parental involvement and school achievement. Positive effects can occur across race, socio economic status (SES), and other sociocultural variables, as previously reported by Epstein (1995).

Effective Parental Involvement

Some researchers have looked at kinds of parental involvement, especially within ethnic and economic subgroups. Others, however, also investigated the effectiveness of types of involvement to determine which ones make the most difference in student achievement. Vandergrift and Greene (1992) believed that effective parental involvement should have two components: parents as supporters of the educational process, and parents as active partners with schools. In addition to defining parental involvement at the school level, Cochran and Dean (1991) stressed the importance of providing examples of effective parental participation in meaningful interactions with children and in decision making.

With regard to effective parental involvement, Epstein (1986) stated, "Research suggests that although parents' educational backgrounds differ, more—and less—educated parents have similar goals as the school for their children's education" (p. 125). Research conducted by Epstein (1984a) with Title I data showed that the most effective parental involvement occurs when teachers involve parents in helping their children with learning activities at home.

Research also has shown that the more intensively parents were involved in their children's learning, the more beneficial the achievement effects. Another finding was that the earlier parents started participating in their children's learning, the more powerful the effects on their children's future achievement (Cotton & Wakelund, 1989). Active parental involvement (parent-child interactions where the child was learning cognitive concepts and skills in a playful, culturally relevant manner) produced greater achievement benefits than passive participation (signing forms, calling the school, attending parent-teacher conferences) (Henderson & Berla, 1994).

Some studies showed that parents were willing to help their child but did not know exactly what to do. In these cases, mediation from the teachers resulted in more effective parental involvement. A survey of 2,317 elementary and middle schools (Dauber & Epstein, 1989) found that the strongest and most consistent predictors of parental involvement at home and at school were the specific school programs or teacher practices that encouraged parental involvement in school and guided parents in how to help their children at home. In this study, parents in general said they wanted to support their children's learning but they wanted the school to show them specific ways to do so.

In a qualitative study of parental involvement, Goldenberg (1987) found that low SES, culturally, and linguistically different families were capable of helping their children learn to read by directly helping with the school curriculum. The study showed that many parents tended to use their own cultural ways of learning while teaching their children at home. Goldenberg stated that although some teachers wanted parents to help their children in ways that were congruent with school instruction, there was no systematic attempt from the school to ask for their help.

When parents received definitive instructions for helping with homework, it resulted in academic improvement. Reese and Gallimore (2000) found that when schools told parents to do specific activities with their children at home to support their children's learning, the parents were very compliant, and the value of their work showed in their children's achievement. For example, a teacher might require that the parent read to the child each evening, even specifying the title of the book and the number of pages to be read. Other literacy activities might also be explained to parents as homework.

Another aspect of school that parents can help with involves the social and cultural climate of the classroom. Scott-Jones (1993) stated that children are socialized toward behaviors that are considered normal and useful within a cultural group. However, these behaviors do not always match expected behaviors in the classroom. With assistance from parents and others, children learn to adapt and use the tools and skills of their own culture as they perform the everyday tasks required in their society. This finding is supported by research done by Rogoff, Gauvain, and Ellis (1984), and it represents a perspective that cannot be overlooked by those working on parental involvement activities.

Parental Attitudes and Sociocultural Factors

Beyond the effects of parental involvement in achievement, other studies have focused on factors such as parents' and teachers' attitudes and stereotypes of parental involvement. Most of the work in this area has been with minority populations.

One of the major researchers who examined attitudes of parents and teachers was Epstein (1995, 2001), who developed a model that she called "spheres of influence." Three overlapping circles represent the family, the community, and the school. According to this framework, the more overlap among the spheres, the more students will be able to achieve in schools in the United States as they are currently structured. For minority and low-income students, there is less overlap among the spheres. This might be due to differences in culture and language, among other factors. Epstein (1987) also discussed opposing assumptions about the role of the school and the family in children's education and how these assumptions affect interactions between teachers and parents. Because the home and the school are sometimes seen as separate entities with different roles but shared responsibilities, Epstein emphasized the need for coordination and cooperation between home and schools. She believed that schools and families should share responsibility for the socialization and education of the child.

Although Epstein's work is highly regarded among researchers and practitioners interested in parental involvement, it has been criticized by some as having a "school centered" focus (Kohl, Lengua, & McMahon, 2000). They and other researchers view parental involvement from a different perspective that considers issues such as who initiates activities (e.g., parents or schools, children or parents) as well as power relationships (e.g., who decides what parents have to learn, how parents teach their children). Others challenge the validity of Epstein's model because it uses terms such as "success" and "achievement," which are culturally defined terms (Banks, 1995; Nieto, 1996, 2002).

Still other research on parental involvement has investigated the topic of sociocultural differences. For example, Henderson and Mapp (2002) found differences in parental involvement across grade levels and across different types of families. For example, low-income and/or minority families tended to be more involved with their children at home than at school. This finding has implications for studies that assess family involvement only through school-based activities.

A survey of parents' attitudes and involvement with school conducted by Chavkin and Williams (1993) found that minority parents were clear about the role they play in their children's education. These parents believed that teachers were responsible for getting parents involved in school and that school districts should develop rules to involve parents. They also wanted the school to help their children understand that parental involvement is important. In addition, parents gave suggestions that might work to help them participate more in the education of their children. Latino parents felt the school should provide them with more information about their children's success in school and that schools and teachers should make parents feel more welcome at school.

African American parents wanted the school to plan more activities when working parents could attend. They would like to have more activities in schools when parents, children, and teachers can all participate, and they wanted to learn more about their children's school success.

A similar survey study (Ritter, Mont-Reynaud, & Dornbusch, 1992) tested the stereotypical view that minority parents, especially of the lower class, were not concerned about their children's education. Parents in the study were divided into two groups, high and low formal education. The researchers found cultural differences among minority groups that might contribute to the varying ways parents relate to the school and how they view an appropriate level of involvement. Lack of proficiency in English also deterred some parents from participating in their children's schools. According to Ritter et al.:

> Less educated parents are not familiar with the curriculum and procedures of American schools; they are less comfortable interacting with the educational system. However, the hesitancy of some minority parents to be involved in the schools does not mean that they do not care about their children's education.
>
> (p. 118)

Based on her many years of work with minority and other parents, Rich (1985) believed that "parents do care about their children's education and want to help" (p. 235). Her experience has been that when parents are involved with children's schools, increased learning takes place, and school achievement scores rise. Although homes might be different from schools, "both home and school continue to be powerful institutions and … the real, best, and only hope for improved education in this country is to unite the educational forces of home, schools, and communities" (p. 236).

Jones (2001) also addressed the issue of parents' attitudes, saying "Forget the notion that parents don't care or won't make time for their children" (p. 4). Not all parents are eager to participate in school activities since some have had negative experiences with schools; others might not be familiar with the culture of American schools. Jones also called for schools to develop strategies that attract families and increase their involvement.

Barriers and Obstacles to Parental Involvement

Sociocultural differences often result in a lower level of involvement for some parents. Unfortunately, teachers and schools frequently equate parents' lack of participation with lack of interest in their children's education. This attitude was challenged by Baker (1999), who involved parents from all religious, ethnic, and SES backgrounds in focus groups. The study found that parents really cared about their children's education, were willing to make time for their children, and wanted to participate in the process. The problem was not so much the parents' attitude as it was other barriers to their involvement.

Moore (1991) sees distance between parents and teachers, lack of teacher training, differences in race and culture, limited views of parental involvement, and the public perception of schools as general barriers to parental involvement. Logistical issues such as lack of time, transportation, and childcare as well as scheduling can be barriers to parental involvement for any sociocultural group (Delgado-Gaitan, 2001; Moles, 1994; Moore, 1991; Scribner, Young, & Pedroza, 1999). Schools might not keep these various factors in mind when planning parental involvement activities.

Other barriers discussed in research studies include parents' level of education and experiences with schools (Moles, 1994). Parents with low educational levels might feel intimidated talking to teachers and uncomfortable supporting their children's learning at home. Carger (1996) found that some parents have had unpleasant experiences when interacting with schools. Other parents might not have been successful in their own education and felt anxiety when dealing with their children's teachers or schools (Hislop, 2000). Ritter et al. (1992) listed similar reasons along with a lack of trust in institutions.

Many of these same barriers were found by the American Association of School Administrators (AASA) (1998) and included: schools with unwelcoming atmospheres; teachers who lack knowledge of how to reach and involve parents; parents who do not understand the value of their involvement; parents who feel vulnerable because they speak a language other than English; parents stressed from their daily life; parents' lack of support (time, childcare, transportation) to get involved; and parents' perception that nothing will change. The Association states, "Any plan to improve parental involvement must address the reasons parents don't get involved" (p. 22).

Similar reasons were discussed by Bright (1996); some parents might not see the value of participation in parental involvement activities. Others have the perception that nothing will change were they to get more involved in their children's education. If their daily life is already stressful, parents might not be willing to add the additional demands of interacting with teachers or school personnel. Although many parents often feel helpless about how to support their children's learning at home (Public Agenda, 1999), this survey also found that most parents today (74%) felt that they were doing more for their children's education than their parents had done for them, and many of them (71%) also wished that they could do more.

Most of the barriers mentioned so far address characteristics of the parents. Barriers also originate from beliefs, perceptions, and attitudes of teachers and administrators toward parents. Liontos (1992) believed that teachers' low expectations for at-risk students and negative communication between the parents and the schools were barriers to parental involvement. Leitch and Tangri (1988) found that lack of planning and lack of mutual understanding appeared to be major barriers to home–school collaboration between junior high teachers and parents.

More specifically, Cochran (1987) stated that a combination of beliefs and assumptions leads administrators, teachers, and other school personnel to see weaknesses rather than strengths, particularly in minority families. This in turn leads to the use of deficit models in parental involvement training that allow participation only by parents who show perceived inadequacies. Cochran called for change whereby parental involvement programs are built upon family strengths, take into account linguistic and cultural differences, and lead to empowerment. Cochran defined empowerment as:

> An interactive process involving mutual respect and critical reflection, through which both people and controlling institutions are changed in ways that provide those people with greater influence over individuals and institutions which are in some ways influencing their efforts to achieve equal status in society.
>
> (p. 109)

Cochran felt it was the responsibility of the school to remove these barriers to parental involvement. Liontos (1992) agreed, saying that it is important for teachers to realize that all families have strengths, many family structures exist, and cultural differences should be validated. The school also needs to understand that parents can learn new strategies to support their children.

Barriers for minority parents might be even more numerous than some realize. Language and cultural barriers are issues that many culturally different parents have to deal with in order to become involved in their children's education. Researchers working with Latino parents (e.g., Chavkin & Gonzalez, 1995; Gibson, 2002; Hislop, 2000) have discussed the problem of communication between teachers and Spanish-speaking parents about their children's behavior when the teachers did not speak Spanish. Also, if interpreters were not available, parents could not always understand what was being said when they attended school meetings (Scribner et al., 1999).

Beyond language, cultural differences can cause problems. Espinosa (1995) found that, although Latino parents from different Spanish-speaking countries might differ in terms of communication styles and sociocultural practices, they all had strong family ties, family loyalty, and an orientation toward community life. She reported that Latinos preferred warm personal interactions, a relaxed sense of time, and informal forms of communication, which were sometimes in conflict with the mainstream style of teachers in American schools. Other research has shown that Latino parents and families were very involved in their children's educational lives, although they did not participate in their children's schooling in traditional ways (Espinosa, 1995; Lopez, 2001; Scribner et al., 1999).

Several core concepts of Latinos are generally not accepted or understood by teachers or schools. Gibson (2002) has found a disconnection between home and school, which was hard for parents to understand. In general, the school did not value the home culture. The concept of "familia," in which the needs of the family come before the needs of the individual (Abi-Nader, 1993), was usually misunderstood by the schools. Also, the idea of cooperation (or collectivism as defined by Trumbull, Rothstein-Fish, Greenfield, & Quiroz, 2001) instilled in Latino families was usually in conflict with the individualism and competitive focus emphasized in schools.

Another concept difference involves perceptions of parental involvement by both teachers and parents. Chavkin and Gonzalez (1995) found that for Latino parents there was a clear difference between the role of the school and the role of the parents in the children's learning. Parents saw their role as one of nurturing and teaching of morals and values, while they expected the school to instill academic knowledge

(Carger, 1996; Chavkin & Gonzalez, 1995; Reese, Balzano, Gallimore, & Goldenberg, 1995; Rodríguez-Brown, 2004). In the Latino culture, teachers are highly respected, and interference with schools might be seen as disrespectful by parents (Chavkin & Gonzalez, 1995; Trumbull et al., 2001).

Recognition of these cultural differences and the barriers they represent leads Rich (1993) to state:

> In some ways, because of minority parents' experiences with schooling, because of how they may still feel about schools and because schools by and large do not have the strategies and the people in place to work with them, minority parents may indeed be harder to reach.
>
> (p. 235)

There are other ways that teachers' attitudes might affect Latino parents. Some researchers (Inger, 1992; Lindle, 1989) have reported a patronizing, distant, or condescending attitude that can leave parents feeling intimidated. A school environment, in which parents felt unwelcome, for whatever reason, limited or inhibited parental involvement (Chavkin, 1989; Scribner et al., 1999). Moles (1994) attributed the problem to a lack of teacher pre-service or in-service training in parental involvement, and in dealing with parents from diverse backgrounds. Even today, few teacher education programs provide training in home–school relations, so it is necessary for schools to provide training in this area.

Despite the barriers, there is a general consensus that schools must address these problems and find ways to increase the involvement of minority parents. According to Cotton and Wakelund (1989):

> Perhaps the most important finding of the research (on parental involvement) ... is that parents of disadvantaged and minority children can and do make a positive contribution to their children's achievement at school, if they receive adequate training and encouragement in the types of parental involvement that can make a difference. Even more significant, the research dispels a popular myth by revealing ... that parents can make a difference regardless of their own levels of education. Indeed, disadvantaged children have the most to gain from parental involvement programs.
>
> (p. 6)

Parental Involvement and Educational Policy

In 1984, the Select Committee on Children, Youth, and Families of the House of Representatives held hearings regarding the role of parents in improving the education of American children. Many researchers and organizations participated in the hearings, including Joyce Epstein, Dorothy Rich, and David Williams. Issues discussed included the types of parental involvement that were most effective, the positive effects on student achievement, the need for teacher training, and the lack of policies in support of parental involvement in learning activities at home.

Twenty years later, current policy issues involve the same topics. Everyone sees the relevance and benefits of parental involvement, but there is still a call for research into how to accomplish it. However, some federal policy guidelines have been developed. For example, schools that receive Title I or other federal funds must spend at least 1% of those funds on parental involvement activities. Also, school districts are required to develop parental involvement policy guidelines in coordination with parents whose children attend their schools. Other state policies have been developed to address issues of parental involvement.

State Policies

A review of the policy for several large states (New York, California, and Tennessee) shows some common trends as states work to fulfill the requirement for parental involvement in their own contexts. Most of the state plans mention implementing and evaluating parental involvement activities, but lack specificity in terms of funding and the nature of the activities to be carried out. Most plans at all levels (state, district, and local school) also list Epstein's (1995) six types of involvement as examples they want to implement.

The state of New York policy (www.emsc.nysed.gov/deputy/NCLB/parents/parents.htm) tells parents how schools will work with them to develop parental involvement policy at the local level. It mentions components for teacher training, parent training, and the development of resource centers. There is no specific information as to any support, accountability guidelines, or how parental involvement programs will be developed, administered, implemented, or evaluated, as mandated under Title I.

California (www.cde.ca.gov/ms/po/policy89–01) has had a state policy for parental involvement since 1984. It requires districts to develop their own policies to implement and evaluate parental involvement at the local school level. It calls for comprehensive and coordinated programs at all grade levels, and it states that the parents and the school have a shared responsibility for the children's education. However, the policy lacks specificity as to funding for these activities and the types of parental involvement that are expected.

In Tennessee (www.state.tn.us/sbe/tnpi.pdf), policy states that the education of children is a shared responsibility and lists the six components included in Epstein's (1995) typology as areas in which parental involvement should occur. Here again, there is no specific information about funding, types of activities, or minimum requirements for parental involvement at the district or school level.

District Policies

An example of policy at the district level is that of the Chicago Public Schools (CPS). The parental involvement policy described on their Web site (www.policy.cps.k12.il.us/documents/801.3.pdf) repeats exactly what the Title I guidelines mandate. There is no mention of the requirement that schools spend at least 1% of Title I funds on parental involvement programs. CPS encourages schools to offer programs in a "feasible way." There is no theoretical framework underlying parental involvement activities, except to say that training should be offered to parents in Title I schools, and information should be provided to parents. Funding and accountability issues are not addressed.

The Baltimore Public Schools' policy is a little more specific in that it calls for positive collaboration between parents and schools (www. bcps. k12.md.us/School_Board/policies/Parent_Involvement.asp). Epstein's (1995) typology for parental involvement is suggested. The policy also calls for a responsive school climate as a way to enhance students' achievement and attendance. There is not much information about parental involvement activities that might occur within a more responsive school climate.

A smaller school district, Palos Verdes, California (www.pvpusd .k12.ca.us) has a policy that is more specific concerning teacher training, but does not list parent training or learning-at-home activities as areas that could increase parents' effectiveness when working with their children.

Parental involvement policy for another small district, Christina, Delaware (1998) (www.christina.k12.de.us/en2/school_board/ parentinvolvement.htm) reads much the same as the state law. Parents must be involved in determining school policies. Epstein's (1995) typology for parental involvement is recommended. The policy supports the implementation of teacher training and encourages parent participation, but does not list specific activities for parents.

Another small district, Federal Way, Washington (www.fwpa.org/info/ family) has adopted a policy that recognizes parents as the "primary" authorities and decision makers in their children's education. The policy statement, based on the Epstein (1995) typology, calls for:

- Schools to develop collaborative relationships between home and school based on high expectations for student achievement and behavior.

- Each school leadership team to develop, implement, and maintain an effective parent/family involvement program that is of interest to parents and students.
- School parental involvement practices that are two-way and include components from the Epstein typology.
- Schools to show a long-term commitment to parental involvement and create permanent structures to support it.
- Schools to be evaluated annually on how they have attained their goals related to parental involvement.

Generally speaking, state, district, and school parental involvement policies seem to be a repeat of the language included in the Title I guidelines, which allows them to be in compliance with the requirement to have a local policy. These policies are decontextualized and very general. It is difficult to see any parent or community input in them. There seems to be some awareness of standards related to parental involvement since several of the policies specify the components of the Epstein typology (1995) as areas to include in a parental involvement policy at different levels. However, most policies are also one-sided in that they talk about teacher training but ignore parent training.

National Organizations

A number of school-related national organizations have developed policies regarding parental involvement. The National PTA (www.pta.org/programs/pfistand.htm) states that schools can use Title I monies for parental involvement activities. The PTA also provides instructions for writing parental involvement policy and a list of possible activities to enhance parents' participation in their children's education.

The Center for Law and Education (CLE) (www.cleweb.org) is more specific about requirements for parental involvement under Title I. It states that schools have to spend at least 1% of the Title I funds on parental involvement, and parents must participate in the process of designing policy. It calls for parents of special education students and English Language Learners to be included in the process. The development of School/Parent Compacts and accompanying responsibilities are described.

Another organization, the AASA, addresses parental involvement policy in a themed issue of *Leader's Edge Newsletter* (AASA, 1998). This issue discusses specifically the role of a superintendent in developing parental involvement policy. It explains that such policies should be more specific than sending memos home. Also discussed are factors that impact parents' participation in school activities and barriers to parental involvement. Another concept emphasized is the need for parents to feel welcome as central to their involvement.

The Association also calls for evaluation of activities, specific goals, parent input, and information that can be sent home to parents. Epstein's (1995) six kinds of parental involvement are listed and referred to as "national standards" for parental involvement because they have been endorsed by as many as 30 organizations.

The relevance of Epstein's typology to parental involvement is also discussed on a page at the Web site of the American School Board (ASB) (www.asbj.com/2001/09/0901coverstory.html). Although the ASB lists the six components in Epstein's model, it also states that not all parental involvement works. Claiming that student achievement is influenced by teacher quality as well as SES and parental involvement, the organization calls for schools to stop finding new ways to blame parents. Instead it recommends a new definition of parental involvement and the design of good and effective programs.

Jesse (1998) also sees a need to redefine parental involvement in order to consider changing families, saying it is not appropriate to define parental involvement the same way for all populations and all contexts. In his report "Increasing Parental Involvement," Jesse cites research (e.g., Hester, 1989; Liontos, 1992) and policy publications that call for new ways to look at families, viewing parents in different roles such as teachers, learners, supporters, and active participants in their children's learning. Jesse's paper also embraces Epstein's typology (1995) for parental involvement, discusses barriers to parental involvement, and addresses the issue of differences between what parents want and what schools think they want or need. He includes several lists of parent activities that fit different paradigms related to parental involvement.

Finally, the North Central Regional Education Laboratory (NCREL) (2004), a research and development laboratory, suggests strategies for improving the quality of parental involvement, such as the enhancement of school climate. Their report calls for the coordination of resources with programs such as Head Start, with family services (not connected directly to the school), and with an active parent-teacher organization (PTO). However, the report does not include possibilities for parents to serve as resources at home and at school. There is also a lack of sensitivity to culturally and linguistically different parents who might not be able or willing to participate in PTO activities.

What all of these policy recommendations lack is an awareness of the need to share knowledge between home and school. From school districts to educational organizations, except for the Jesse (1998) paper, there seems to be no awareness of the many possibilities for parental involvement in children's learning at home and school. Most of the documents do not contain a definition of parental involvement that fits the needs of parents in today's world. What is being called parental involvement from a policy perspective is mostly a superficial way to address the issue. In spite of guidelines regarding parental involvement in government funded programs, there is very little in terms of policy that schools and associations are doing to enhance or even define parental involvement in relation to the varied needs of parents. School districts and schools do not have specific plans of action for parental involvement; nor are they using Title I for parent training. There appears to be the belief that simply training teachers to involve parents in their children's education is going to make a difference. Parent training is not a priority in parental involvement.

If schools want parents to be involved in their children's education, parents need to be taught how to support learning both at home and at school. They need to know the expectations of the school and the teachers. They must feel welcome and wanted in the school. This is even more important for culturally and linguistically different parents who are often hesitant or insecure about visiting their child's school but are curious about what classrooms look like and how they function in the United States.

What is needed is policy, which although general, allows for the needs of diverse populations in schools today with lists of specific activities at the state, district, and local school levels. Parents and the community must be consulted in policy development. Title I schools should be held accountable for the requirement to provide parent training, but they often need help to develop a plan for such training. There also must be accountability through the evaluation of activities, beyond parents' attendance at school-centered activities.

Resources

Many of the organizations mentioned in the previous section recognize the advantages of enhancing parental involvement and have called for more accountability in this endeavor. These organizations are also aware of recommended standards for parental involvement. The next step is planning, in a coordinated manner, parental involvement activities that are specific to the communities and schools being served. The development of a parental involvement program must be seen as an effort that requires not only teacher training and participation but also parent training. An effective program necessitates parents and teachers working together and learning from each other for the benefit of children. Finally, there must be accountability and evaluation of current practices as a means to continual improvement. The following pages include a discussion of possible resources to make parental involvement a feasible reality.

Partnerships

A number of partnerships, models, and frameworks have been developed to address the needs of schools and districts that are developing a program for parental involvement. General aspects and features of each are discussed as well as strengths and weaknesses.

National Network of Partnership Schools

Epstein (1992) and her associates at Johns Hopkins University have designed the National Network of Partnership Schools in support of the development and implementation of two-way, home–school connections, or partnerships among parents, communities, schools, and teachers. The conceptual framework underlying the partnership is based on Epstein's research (1984a, 1986, 1995), and includes the six types of parental involvement discussed earlier. The National Network provides participants with sample practices, a discussion of possible challenges, possible results for their work, and planning and evaluation tools. There is no prescribed plan for action to be followed by everyone. Rather, partnerships require a local action team which includes parents and community, as well as school personnel (teachers, administrators), who work together in designing and implementing a plan of activities that is contextualized to their setting.

The Network also makes its members aware of the need to fund and evaluate their activities through federal, state, local, and private sources. As part of the development process, members of the Network also become familiar with the steps necessary to guide the work of individual partnerships. District and state leaders are asked to facilitate the attainment of partnership goals.

What is commendable about the Network's partnership procedures is the focus on the process of developing partnerships and the need for parents, communities, teachers, and schools to collaborate in determining a course of action specific to their context and their needs. However, one does not see in the recommendations any provisions for equal influences from both home and school in the partnership's decision making, activities, and/or plan of action. Rather, activities as described are centered on the school and run by school personnel. Procedures also seem to be school centered. Parents and community should have a more active role in the activities of the partnership. There are so many things that school personnel could learn from parents and community people were they to work together and plan activities as real partners.

National Coalition for Parental Involvement in Education

Another organization that has designed procedures to develop partnerships between home and school is the National Coalition for Parental Involvement in Education (www.ncpie.org). Their Web site describes a framework for parental involvement, which includes components to support communication, school activities, home activities, life-long learning, advocacy, shared governance, and collaboration with community organizations. These components correlate with Epstein's (1995) typology for parental involvement. The general procedures as described on the Web site do not emphasize a process. Also, for each component, there is a list of what each parent and school can do separately rather than a requirement for interaction between partners (parents and teachers) in the process of developing partnership activities. In a true partnership, those involved collaborate to design programs and activities in support of common goals.

In addition, many of the activities described in the components list are traditional ones that already occur in schools. There seems to be an imbalance in the process which favors the role of the schools. Issues of diversity, differences in cultures, languages, literacies, and possible barriers to parental involvement are not addressed. In the learning-at-home component, parents are not encouraged to participate in their children's learning per se, but in helping them develop good study habits, in supervising their homework, and ensuring regular bedtimes and school attendance. There is no recognition that parents are the children's first teachers, nor that parents have a wealth of knowledge that they can share with their children at home in cultural ways that might be different from school but still contribute to learning and possibly to school achievement.

Although it is important and necessary for teachers to show parents how to support children's learning at home, the recommendations given to teachers in their work with parents are very much based on what other people think parents need to do. There is no opportunity for parents and teachers to share ideas and make decisions about how to support children's learning at home in ways that are culturally relevant but also in some way congruent with what children are learning at school.

The NCPIE framework for the work of partnerships seems to be guided by a deficit perspective toward their life-long learning component. Possible activities for parents as life-long learners include basic adult education, job training, and parenting education. There is no recognition that parental involvement activities should be directed toward all parents, rather than those whom schools feel are uneducated or lacking skills. In developing activities for the life-long learning component, context and parent input are necessary to make the program relevant to all participants.

Identified life-long learning activities for teachers include learning about the community culture and values. This is a good start, but activities must include more specific ways in which teachers learn and share expectations with parents, and where both learn from each other, in a trustful and respectful environment, as they collaborate in the education of children.

The NCPIE Web site includes several examples of partnerships in action. Two of them (Passport for Students' Success and East Coast Technical Assistant Center) include workshops or conferences for parents but no evidence of partnership or collaboration in the design and content of the training. It is difficult to determine whether the topics would be of interest to parents and whether their needs or desires are fulfilled, as they try to support their children's learning at home in ways that are culturally relevant.

Parents of Children of African Descent

Another example, Parents of Children of African Descent (PCAD) is a program for parents of high school students. At the request of the school principal, parents designed an intervention plan for students who might otherwise drop out of school. The plan included the creation of a learning community within the high school. This program demonstrates a real partnership in that the school and the home collaborate in planning activities to support their children's learning and keep them in school.

Network of Educators on the Americas

A different model for partnerships between home and school is called Tellin' Stories: Connecting Parents, Schools, and Communities, developed by the Network of Educators on the Americas (NECA) (n.d.). The model is based on the organization's belief that "families, schools, and communities must be involved as purposeful partners in the education process" (p. 1). Another tenet is that stories have the power to connect people from diverse backgrounds in order to pass on valuable information and to organize for collective action. Tellin' Stories includes school-based workshops for families and school personnel that serve as forums to bridge differences and achieve shared goals. One goal of the program is to improve parents' access to schools and to broaden parents' roles in all the components of Epstein's (1995) typology for parental involvement. It is expected that parents who assume their roles will have the power to collaboratively transform schools.

This model of parental involvement requires a six-step process: community building, gathering information and developing skills, identifying and prioritizing concerns, taking action, collaborating, and evaluating. The model is contextualized to each school or district setting and involves collaboration between school personnel and parents. Schools are encouraged to develop a school culture relevant to the children and one that encourages parents to develop self-efficacy, as they support their children's learning at home and at school.

The National Center for Family Literacy

A model for parental involvement that is specific to literacy has been developed by the National Center for Family Literacy (NCFL) (1995). The model is described on the Center's Web site (www.famlit.org/FamilyLiteracyServices/index.cfm) and is discussed further in Chapter 2. Four components are included: children's education, parent time, parent-and-child together, and adult education. These components are congruent with U.S. government legislation (Workforce Investment Partnership Act [1998], commonly called the Adult Education and Family Literacy Act), and parallel with those required for Even Start Program funding. The model comes out of a deficit perspective in determining which parents and families are allowed to participate in the program. Effectiveness of services is measured by the intensity (defined as number of hours), length of time, and integration of the four components of the model.

Approaches used for training in this model are top-down, based on what the developers feel participants' families need to learn in order to become economically self-sufficient. There is no room for sharing parents' knowledge or cultural ways of teaching and learning, either as a way to support children's learning or as a steppingstone to new learning opportunities. From the developers' perspective, the model creates partnerships for learning that support teachers, schools, parents, and children, but as an intervention, the approach is unidirectional, and its ultimate goal is family self-sufficiency, rather than the enhancement of ways in which parents share knowledge with their children and participate actively in their education.

The Harvard Family Research Project

Although described as a school-community partnership project, The Harvard Family Research Project (HFRP) (www.gseweb.harvard.edu/hfrp/projects/family.html) is basically an organization that provides resources to policy makers and educators in support of the development of parental involvement as a field of research, policy, and practice.

Through the research, the project intends to strengthen professional development for those who work with children, youth, and families. The project also provides assistance in evaluation practices in support of effective and sustainable partnerships among parents, schools, and communities. In some ways, the HFRP works in partnership with organizations interested in parental involvement, rather than with parents or schools. Its role in these partnerships is the development of a knowledge base to support parental involvement programs, and also the training of teachers who could reach out to families. Information provided by HFRP benefits policy makers and school personnel and, only indirectly, parents and children. Their Web site is not specific as to how culture, language, race, and ethnicity are addressed in their work, or how they approach issues of diversity in their research and publications for school personnel.

General Guidelines for Partnerships

In any partnership, one of the most important considerations is that shared responsibilities are designed so that parents and the community have an equal voice with teachers and administrators in developing and implementing parental involvement plans and training. Good partnerships require that participants trust and respect each other in order for real collaboration to occur (Wagner & Spiker, 2001). Partnerships should support a home–school connection that is two-way—parents learn about the school's expectations for their children, about schooling and what takes place in classrooms, while teachers learn about families' cultures and languages, parents' expectations for their children, and the cultural ways of sharing knowledge that they use with their children at home. Parents should be able to share with teachers their cultural capital, and teachers should learn to see this capital as a resource, rather than a deficit as it relates to children's learning.

Any intervention in support of parents' involvement at school and/or at home should be based on the strengths of the families involved, and be open to all who want to participate. Currently, most school interventions in parental involvement are based on perceived weaknesses or deficit perspectives of the target populations to be served by the programs (Rich, 1993). It is only when families show deficits, which in many ways are merely differences from the mainstream, that they are invited to participate. Yet, parents usually do not see themselves, their language, culture, race, and ethnicity represented and/or acknowledged in intervention training activities.

An effective intervention program must also prepare teachers to work with parents, particularly those who are culturally and linguistically different. Teachers should be trained in ways to connect with parents to share experiences and expectations with them. Visits to neighborhoods and families around the school could serve to challenge some of the stereotypes that parents and teachers might have about each other. It could also lower the anxiety that parents, as well as teachers, might have about dealing with each other, and thus open real communication between home and school. Once mutual respect has been established, parental involvement training activities could be designed in ways that are relevant to the setting and those (parents and teachers) involved in the partnership. After a specific plan is developed, issues of accountability can be discussed. Evaluation of partnership effectiveness should be carried out yearly, and the findings should lead to improvements in the activities designed for parents and teachers to learn from each other, as they support children's learning, both at home and at school.

Resources Available from Organizations

The projects described above are called partnerships, and they serve different constituencies in the development of home–school connections. Some programs coordinate their work with parents and/or teachers, while others develop their own models, activities, evaluation, and/or research agendas, according to what the project personnel believe is needed for parents to get involved. Some programs use already existing models and commercial resources to support their work; others make adaptations of existing resources and materials to their own situations and contexts.

There are several organizations that provide resources to support parental involvement activities. Although some resources can be adapted to different contexts and populations, others are pre-packaged. It is the responsibility of both parents and school personnel to find out which resources meet their needs best and are aligned most closely with their goals and their contexts. Some of the better known organizations that provide resources are described next.

Megaskills

Megaskills Education Center of the Home School Institute (www.MegaSkillsHSI.org) is a resource center that offers services and specific programs to schools in support of their parental involvement program efforts. The Web site describes their programs as geared toward the academic and character development of children. The Center offers training for different constituencies; MegaSkills materials are specific to children at different grade levels. One of the concerns is that it is a pre-packaged program developed to fit all kinds of families and learners.

Although the program is described as acknowledging the strengths of families and their children, it is hard to understand how a program designed a priori can fit distinct and unique contexts, and take into account the different strengths that diverse families bring to the learning situation. In terms of character education, it is not clear how a program can serve the needs of families from varied cultural backgrounds that might have different beliefs about how to educate their children in regards to morals and values.

Another concern is the existence of translated materials to serve the needs of non-English speaking families. The use of translations is questionable since not all concepts can be translated to convey the same meaning and intent as the original language. It is not clear who chooses this program for parental involvement, but since it is a skills-based learning program, the school probably makes the decision. There is no awareness of how the program might be aligned with cultural ways of learning at home and the role of the parents' discourses (Gee, 1999) and multiliteracies (The New London Group, 1996) as they work with their children at home.

Parents as Teachers

The Parents as Teachers National Center, Inc. (www.patnc.org) offers a model to train parents as teachers who can promote intellectual development in their children. This is a widely used model for parental involvement. One concern is how or whether the program allows for adaptations to parents' strengths, cultures, and knowledge. It is unclear whether project activities are designed to allow diversity in ways to teach children, or whether the program activities align with home-like learning as opposed to school-like learning principles. From the description provided, it seems the intent of the program is to create an intervention to teach parents how to teach children in a mainstream manner. In a diverse society, that is no longer an option.

The Center for the Development of Schools and Communities

Another possible resource is the Center for the Development of Schools and Communities (e-mail: cdsc1@aol.com), which offers informational materials for both teachers and parents on topics such as Exploring your Community, Working with Families and Communities, and How to Help your Child Succeed in School. These publications or presentations are directed to either parents or teachers. There is no attempt to allow these two constituencies to learn from each other and/or to collaborate in their common endeavors as they support children's learning. Since some of the materials are workbooks, it is not clear how parents' knowledge, cultures, etc. could be taken into account in the learning situation. There are questions about efforts to contextualize the training to each context or situation, the role of parents in the training of teachers in a specific community, and possible interaction and learning between parents and teachers about expectations and cultural ways of learning. The model does not reflect an awareness of the relevance of the home–school connection in the development of partnerships between home and schools.

The Center for Parent Leadership

Another organization, the Center for Parent Leadership at the Prichard Committee (www.centerforparentleadership.org), offers resources for parents to learn about the No Child Left Behind Act (United States, 2001) and how it affects them and their children. The organization also offers a workshop and training guide for parents, communities, and educators to fortify their relationships and to work together toward a common goal of enhancing students' learning. However, it is not clear how the training provides support for those activities in diverse settings. In other words, how is the material discussed in the workshop to be successful in a community where there are existing barriers to parental involvement; where there is no trust or respect for each other; or where schools and parents do not collaborate?

The Parent Institute

A source for printed materials is The Parent Institute (n.d.) (www.parent-institute.com) which offers booklets, newsletters, and a Web site full of ideas for parental involvement. However, these publications were developed from a top-down perspective (what someone thought parents or teachers should know). The materials are generic, although schools can ask for them to be personalized with district identification during printing. It is hard to predict how publications like this are aligned with the needs of a community or a school, and whether the activities are relevant to all parents in the school.

The National Parent Teacher Association

Publications are also available from the National Parent Teacher Association (www.pta.org/parentinvolvement/standards/index.asp), which offers several booklets on parental involvement. The PTA adopted Epstein's (1995) typology of parental involvement as their standards and has published a guide for implementing them in school communities. The guide includes tips for developing parent/family involvement programs.

One of the special features of the publication is a Parental Involvement Schools for Excellence link on their Web site where schools across the country report how they have implemented the six standards. The guide also provides questions that districts might use to identify strengths and weaknesses in their parental involvement program. It is expected that the guide will be used by all stakeholders (parents, teachers, administrators, support staff, and community leaders) in the creation of parental involvement programs. By allowing different stakeholders into the development, planning, and implementations of the programs, schools can develop effective programs that are relevant to everyone involved.

The National Association of Elementary School Principals

Information of interest to principals on how to develop school communities is available from the National Association of Elementary School Principals (NAESP) (n.d.). The publications are generic, address only the needs of school principals, and include such topics as: how to deal with parents; how to include every parent in school activities; how to reach out to families; and how to have parents on your side. None of the materials listed seem to deal with issues of culturally and linguistically different parents or issues of diversity in general.

Suggestions for Use

In using resources such as the ones described above, it is necessary for schools to think about how the materials and their contents are relevant to the population (parents, teachers, school personnel) participating in their parental involvement activities. Resources that are used should allow the school to contextualize any training and activities to their school setting. Another important aspect to consider is the importance of recognizing the strengths of families, their culture, language, and literacies as starting points for further training and partnerships in support of children's learning. Personally, in working with parents who do not know English well, I would advocate adaptation of materials rather than translations. I would ask parents to review the materials for relevance and usability in the school community. It is important for school personnel and families to work in partnership as they strive toward a common goal—that of supporting children's learning both at home and at school.

Conclusion

Recent research has shown the effectiveness of parental involvement on school achievement (Desimone, 1999; Henderson & Mapp, 2002; Reynolds et al., 2001). Barriers to feasible and effective parental involvement have been identified (Hislop, 2000; Liontos, 1992; Moles, 1994). Policies are in place at the state, district, and local school levels in support of parental involvement. Successful and effective partnerships have been developed that recognize differences and value the resources of the community and families (Epstein, 1995, 2001). Programs and resources for the development of programs are available from a variety of sources. Now is the time to begin making major changes in current conceptions and practices of parental involvement and making shared responsibilities a priority in order to make two-way, home–school connections work effectively.

Chapter 2

Family Literacy

Introduction

The previous chapter dealt with issues related to parental involvement. Epstein (1995) describes a typology of parental involvement that includes six categories: parenting, communicating, volunteering, learning at home, decision making, and collaboration with the community. This chapter looks at the category of learning at home, which includes family literacy among other activities. According to Epstein (1987), learning at home is the type of parental involvement that contributes the most to school achievement.

Definition of Family Literacy

The term family literacy, like parental involvement, has different meanings when viewed from certain perspectives. Some define family literacy as programs that support families from low educational and low economic backgrounds to help them become self-sufficient, get jobs, and also support their children's learning. For example, McCoy and Watts (1992) describe family literacy as a "community-based initiative designed to break the cycle of illiteracy" (p. 1) among parents, children, and families. The National Center for Family Literacy (1995) defines family literacy as an intergenerational program which integrates adult literacy instruction and early childhood education for undereducated families. For their purposes, family is defined in a broad sense and in relation to the development of programs that empower families toward self-sufficiency.

Similar views are shared by several others: Community Literacy (Moneyhun, 1997; Peck, Flowers, & Higgins, 1995), who use the term family literacy as it relates mostly to community-based adult literacy programs; and intergenerational literacy (Paratore, 1993, 2001), which describes the process by which literacy practices in one generation influence the next.

Another perspective, however, describes family literacy as home literacy practices that involve oral and written texts in support of children's literacy learning, not as a program directed to help adults become self-sufficient. This view recognizes the literacy knowledge that families already possess and addresses the need to expand the home repertoire of literacy practices. Definitions from this perspective are based on what is necessary for culturally and linguistically different families to learn in order to better support their children's learning in school in the United States.

Using this perspective, Morrow, Paratore, and Tracey (as cited in Morrow, 1995) have developed the following definition:

> Family literacy encompasses the ways parents, children, and extended family members use literacy at home and in their community. Sometimes, family literacy occurs naturally during the routines of daily living and helps adults and children "get things done." These events might include using drawings or writings to share ideas; composing notes or letters to communicate messages; making lists; reading; and following directions; or sharing stories and ideas through conversations, reading, and writing. Family literacy may be initiated purposefully by a parent or may occur spontaneously as parents and children go about the business of their daily lives. Family literacy activities may also reflect the ethnic, racial, or cultural heritage of the families involved.
>
> (pp. 7–8)

The International Reading Association's Family Literacy Commission takes a similar stance on family literacy and has adapted this definition for use on their Web site (www.reading.org/downloads/parents/p6_ 1045_family.pdf) and in publications.

However, not everyone agrees with this definition. De Bruin-Parecki, Paris, and Seidenberg (1996) criticize it as "a general and vague description of family literacy without theoretical foundations or means of implementation" (p. 1). Others believe that the concept of family literacy should be open, allowing researchers or program developers to create an operational definition that matches their own purposes.

In addition to defining family literacy, program developers or researchers are responsible for developing a theoretical framework in support of their research and programs. Just as there is no common definition, there is no one theoretical framework that underlies all research and program development in family literacy. Rather, existing family literacy programs follow one of the perspectives described above.

The definition of family literacy for the purposes of this book includes literacy practices that occur at home and in the community as parents and children engage in activities which support literacy learning in ways that are natural to the home situation and to the cultural ways of learning practiced at home. These activities support not only literacy learning for the whole family but also the cognitive development of the children.

Research on Family Literacy

Studies of Emergent Literacy

It is widely recognized that children acquire basic cognitive and linguistic skills within the context of the family (Heath, 1983). Children's literacy development begins at birth and is supported by the home and the community environment. A positive home literacy environment has an impact on children's success in school and in life (Heath, 1983; Morrow, 1995; Taylor & Dorsey-Gaines, 1988). Emergent literacy has been explored by researchers such as Taylor and Dorsey-Gaines, who examined the effects of parents' efforts in support of early literacy learning even when their educational levels were low; and Teale and Sulzby (1986), who described the role of parent-child interactions with books and how these interactions affected children's emergent literate behaviors and literacy learning.

Some research on the influence of family literacy on children's emergent literacy relies on the principle of transfer whereby skills and behaviors are transmitted from parent to child during activities such as book reading. This research has shown that children learn concepts of print (Clay, 1979), letters (Burguess, 1982), and characteristics of written registers (Purcell-Gates, 1988) through book readings. Such findings have led to interventions in which parents receive books from school to support their children's early literacy learning. Parents also are encouraged to have books, letters, newspapers, and shopping lists at home in an effort to enhance the home literacy environment.

According to Snow and Tabors (1996), however, literacy is more than print skills acquired in a print-rich environment. Television programs such as *Sesame Street* have influenced the background knowledge (social skills, phonics, phonemic awareness, and vocabulary) that most children have before they start school today. Currently, literacy acquisition is seen as a more complex process than before and, therefore, family literacy practices need to be expanded and diversified, especially for emergent readers and writers.

In addition, over time, researchers have expanded the definition of literacy materials used at home to include not only books and magazines (Anderson, Wilson, & Fielding, 1988) but also more functional materials such as notes, bills, and lists (Delgado-Gaitan, 1987; Taylor

& Dorsey-Gaines, 1988). For example, Delgado-Gaitan (1987) discovered that although the parents she studied had little schooling and they did not see themselves as readers, they used written texts such as newspapers, children's schoolbooks, and letters from relatives as part of their daily life.

Research on Literacy Learning at Home

Goodman (1986) describes literacy as a cultural practice. Whether parents simply transmit knowledge, model literacy behaviors, or engage children in meaningful literacy activities, children learn the cultural literacy of the home (Beals, De Temple, & Dickinson, 1994; Dyson, 2003). According to Quezada and Nickse (1993):

> Sharing books in families, when appropriately undertaken, sets a pattern for talking together about things and ideas, and adds to the pleasure of each other's company. Through shared activities the social uses of literacy are incorporated along with orientation to concepts about books and print materials, and the cognitive tasks of asking and answering questions which are so important to the children's school success.
>
> (p. 7)

This quote reflects a "mainstream" perspective toward family literacy and highlights the importance of learning that occurs at home. Some research has looked at the literacy practices of non-mainstream groups. The work of Taylor (1983) and Taylor and Dorsey-Gaines (1988) showed that even parents with low educational levels engage in literacy activities at home, although it might be for different purposes than mainstream parents. In their study, Taylor and Dorsey-Gaines (1988) found that "families use literacy for a wide variety of purposes (social, technical, and aesthetic purposes), for a wide variety of audiences, and in a wide variety of situations" (p. 202). However, this broader view of family literacy is often criticized because of the belief that not all families exhibit literacy practices that lead to early literacy learning (Purcell-Gates, 1995).

Cultural Differences in Family Literacy

Paratore and Harrison (1995) explained that "literacy practices are present in all families, but that these practices are sometimes incongruent with the use of literacy in schools" (p. 516). When children start school, incongruent family practices can result in discontinuities between learning at home and the expectations of a school curriculum that is designed to serve mainstream populations.

Research on how families practice literacy at home has examined cultural and linguistic variations in ways that parents support literacy learning at home. Carger (1996), Delgado-Gaitan (1987), Goldenberg, Reese, and Gallimore (1992), Heath (1983), and more recently Rogers (2001, 2003) have found that culturally and/or linguistically different families supported the literacy development of their children in ways that differed from those of the mainstream population. For example, Goldenberg et al. (1992) described how Latino parents tended to favor discrete skills such as teaching letter naming and letter/sound correspondences as they "taught" literacy to their children. Heath (1983) described how culturally different families from communities only a few miles apart provided their children with different opportunities for literacy learning at home, neither of which reflected fully the expectations of middle-class families or of the school. While parents in one community focused on teaching their children about letters and sounds, parents in another community modeled reading, relying mostly on Bible stories. The expectation of schools was that parents would provide their children with both types of experiences.

Rogers (2001, 2002) described learning situations at home where children learned concepts in different ways than at school and which were not recognized as such by teachers. The African American family that she studied was rich in written literacy usage, but the differences between home and school literacy practices did not allow the daughter opportunities to display her literacy knowledge. As a result, she was placed in a special education class. This family situation was compounded by the fact that, as a child, the mother had experienced failure in the same school system.

The findings mentioned above contrast with the results of studies with middle-class parents who tended to share stories for entertainment and conversation rather than to teach literacy (Baker, Sonnenschein, Serpell, Fernandez-Fein, & Scher, 1994).

Effects of Cultural Differences in Family Literacy

Since families show cultural differences in their purposes for literacy, the ways in which they use literacy in the home, and in their levels of literacy, it follows that children often arrive at school with varying understandings of and experiences with literacy. Some children have had positive literacy models and many opportunities to develop oral language skills that support higher-order literacy learning (Beals et al., 1994; Dyson, 2003). Others have attained knowledge and developed literacy skills that are useful for getting things done in the home and community but that do not contribute to the kind of literacy learning that takes place in school (Dyson, 2003; Gee, 1999; Rogers, 2001).

These differences in family literacy practices have been shown to influence students' achievement. Children who did well in school usually had ways of learning that matched those of the mainstream teacher (Purcell-Gates, 1995; Taylor, 1983; Teale & Sulzby, 1986). These ways of learning were also reflected in the school curriculum and classroom practices, such as the kinds of questions teachers typically ask (Heath, 1983). In addition, mainstream parents, through extended discourse at home, helped their children develop oral language skills that are precursors to vocabulary and discourse skills and that correlate with school success (Beals et al., 1994). Research showed that children whose home oral discourse and literacy experiences were reflected in the curriculum and valued by the school were the ones who benefited the most from what they learned at home and also had an easier transition into schooling (Gee, 1999; Purcell-Gates, 1995; Teale, 1986). Usually, these children were from middle-class homes.

Children from homes where literacy practices did not match those of the mainstream teacher and classroom often experienced academic difficulties due to discontinuities and incongruence between learning at home and learning at school (Delgado-Gaitan, 1987; Gladsden, 1996; Moll, 1992, 1998). Most recently, the work of Gutiérrez and Rogoff (2003) and Rogers (2001, 2002) has described cultural ways of learning that support children's learning at home but not at school. This work is confirmed by that of Dyson (2003) who described the road to literacy as not being the same for all children. According to Gee (1999), culturally and linguistically different children have to learn the secondary discourse of schooling in order to succeed in that setting. For these children, the school discourse is usually very different from the primary discourse learned and practiced at home.

Unfortunately, schools, and teachers in particular, do not value literacy knowledge acquired at home and in the community when it differs from the ways mainstream children learn at home. Teachers do not seem to understand that children who have to learn a secondary discourse at school are able to function in different discourse settings and might have more cognitive flexibility, which could strengthen their school learning (Gee, 1999).

Implications of Cultural Differences

In general, research findings which indirectly or directly address issues of learning at home have implications in several areas. There are implications for the use of specific curricula and methodologies that are sensitive to a diverse student population. There are implications for teacher training programs, such as information on diverse cultural and linguistic ways of learning and the need for teachers to recognize, accept, and use what children learn at home as starting points for new learning at school. There are also implications for schools and their connections with parents. According to Epstein (1986), schools have not done much to alleviate problems related to the discontinuities between home and school learning. Epstein believes that schools have to stop blaming parents for not taking an interest in their child's education and instead start showing parents specific ways that they can support their children's school learning, both before and after their children start school. This does not mean telling parents that what they teach their children about literacy is irrelevant or unimportant. Rather, it means the addition of new literacy repertoires which families could share with their children using their own discourse and cultural ways.

Finally, there are implications that inform the practice and development of family literacy programs. The need for parents to practice new literacy learning activities in addition to what they already do with their children at home and congruent with what is expected in schools has given rise to the development of family literacy programs. Delgado-Gaitan's (1993) research provided evidence that programs that are directed toward culturally and linguistically diverse families empower parents to learn more about schools and school literacy. Furthermore, through family literacy programs, parents can gain confidence in their relationships with teachers and the schools, and children can benefit from new and additional literacy interactions at home.

Family Literacy Programs

Family literacy programs have become a hallmark in the process of helping parents understand their important role as their children's first teachers and the need to make connections to schools. Such programs began to appear in the late 1980s and early 1990s, supported by researchers such as Gladsden (1994), Delgado-Gaitan (1987), and Heath (1983). The purposes of the programs were to provide a connection between home and school, and to mediate the incongruence between what is learned about literacy at home and what is expected at school. Delgado-Gaitan (1993) stated that "organized efforts are necessary ... to provide parents with explicit knowledge about schools and how the educational system operates" (p. 140).

Although the original programs used parents' knowledge and ways of teaching and learning in their design (Gladsden, 1994), there are a number of models based on varying assumptions about families and their literacy needs. A look at ways of categorizing programs and the underlying theoretical assumptions helps to clarify these issues.

Classification

Family literacy programs can have different formats and purposes or serve different populations. One of the most common ways to classify family literacy programs was developed by Nickse (1989), who identified programs by type of participant (adults and/or children), and the degree of intervention, which refers to whether both the child and the adult are together for all components of the program or for only some of them. Services are defined as direct or indirect, where "primary" participants receive direct services and "secondary" participants benefit indirectly from the program. Following this framework, Nickse defined four types of programs.

Type 1 programs include direct services to adults and pre-school aged children. This type is exemplified by the model developed by the National Center for Family Literacy (1995). Through this model parents attend literacy instruction, parenting education sessions, and "parent and child together" activities. Children take part in a structured early childhood or pre-school program.

Type 2 programs indirectly affect both parents and children and are developed to promote the use of literacy for enjoyment. Although there is no curriculum sequence, the programs include a set of literacy enrichment activities such as storytelling, book talks, and library activities. Type 2 programs are usually organized by public libraries or they might be part of after-school activities in the public schools. There is no national or recognized model since each program is developed locally.

Type 3 programs usually offer direct services to adults, but the services indirectly affect children. This type of program includes literacy sessions where parents learn ways to share literacy with their children through storybook reading and/or other literacy related behaviors, as well as English language instruction. Children do not participate in activities regularly. Sometimes goals for Type 3 programs are to support adult literacy learning as a way for adults to influence their children's literacy development. Such is the case of the English Family Literacy Program from the University of Massachusetts at Boston (Auerbach, 1989). Other programs emphasize teaching parents ways to support their children's literacy learning at home through activities such as shared book readings (Intergenerational Literacy Program [ILP], Paratore, 2001) or through a variety of literacy activities such as language interaction activities, language modeling through book readings and games, and learning to connect with schools and teachers (Project FLAME, Rodríguez-Brown, 2004).

Finally, Type 4 family literacy programs are planned for children to be the primary recipients of services. Parents might be invited to participate but do not receive direct services. Some of the programs currently offered under Early Reading First fall in this category. Although there are general guidelines to follow, each district develops its own program.

Family literacy programs also can be defined as group-based, home-based, or a combination of the two (NCFL, 1995). Some programs are identified as parent workshops or discussions while others are called homework clubs. Programs can be classified according to the literacy enhancement services they offer to adults in low-income, low-literacy families (English as a second language classes, basic skills) or by the institutions where they are based (library vs. school programs).

Program Assumptions

Regardless of the typology used, the main difference among programs today is the way they perceive families and their needs, particularly families who are culturally and linguistically different from the mainstream. Family literacy programs are seen as interventions in support of parents' and/or children's learning, either alone or together, and in a home or community environment. There are two philosophical viewpoints that are based on how families and their needs are perceived— deficit and enrichment—one of which underlies each program's design and the nature of the program's activities. The contrasts in viewpoints warrant a closer look at each.

Deficit Perspective

Auerbach (1995) suggested that most of the programs that teach parents about successful, mainstream, child-parent interaction patterns and that supplement existing home materials and literacy strategies are based on a "deficit" model of learning. Programs that are developed for use with low-income, low-education families described as "at-risk" are based on the belief that children from these families and/or culturally different families are not provided with enough literacy learning opportunities at home. In addition, the opportunities that parents do provide for their children do not resemble mainstream literacy behaviors. To supplement the perceived "deficit," a school or another organization designs a program based on what the developers feel the families should be doing with their children at home in order to support their achievement in the mainstream school. Parents are expected to learn how to support their children's literacy learning at home in ways that resemble mainstream ways of learning, and which are congruent with the school curriculum and the school culture. Usually parents are taught directly about activities, such as shared reading, which resemble activities carried out in mainstream classrooms so that they can practice similar activities with their children at home. Mostly through home visits, parents are instructed in new ways to teach literacy to their children at home before the children start school and once they are in school.

Programs based on the deficit model offer comprehensive family services, which include adult education, children's early education, parent-child training, and parenting. Although the programs are identified as family literacy, their focus is not specifically parents and children interacting and learning about literacy at home, but rather parents training for employment and self-sufficiency. The program developers believe that parents who are able to work also provide a better home environment for their children, which in turn improves children's school success.

Because the source of funding for many of these types of programs in the United States is the federal government, data collected for evaluation purposes of deficit model literacy programs are basically for accountability of the program rather than to inform the field. Duration and intensity of services is what matters when considering the success of a program. Parental self-sufficiency is also seen as a measure of success.

Better known programs in this category include the Kenan Family Literacy model, which is used by the National Center for Family Literacy (1995) and the Even Start Family Literacy model. These programs are currently funded through Even Start and through adult education initiatives covered under the Workforce Investment Act of 1998.

Family literacy programs developed from the "deficit" perspective have been criticized for ignoring the literacy events that occur naturally in most homes and also for ignoring what families bring to the learning situation rather than using this knowledge as a steppingstone to new knowledge (Auerbach, 1995; Taylor & Dorsey-Gaines, 1988). These programs do not see the need to value different ways of learning at home and do not take into account what children might have already learned. Since the discourses and/or languages used at home and the cultural ways of learning are not valued, this perspective considers the differences to be detrimental to children's literacy learning and school success. For the most part, the parent-child learning component does not take advantage of what parents could offer to the learning situation or the cultural ways of learning and/or discourses used at home. Parents are never asked for input and/or are not allowed to share literacy in ways that are relevant to the family.

Enrichment Perspective

The second perspective for the development of family literacy programs is the enrichment perspective that is based on principles of sociocultural learning. For most of these programs, family literacy is defined as learning at home in ways that are culturally relevant to the families. For example, parents might share books, tell stories, and encourage children to draw to express their understanding of the world around them. Programs that follow a sociocultural perspective accept and celebrate the literacy activities that parents already share with their children (Gutiérrez & Rogoff, 2003). These programs are aware of and respect cultural and linguistic differences that participants bring into the program as well as the differences in discourse and cultural ways of learning between home and school (Gee, 1999; Rogers, 2001, 2002). They design activities that use "funds of knowledge" (Moll & Greenberg, 1990) from the community as resources to new learning.

Enrichment programs allow parents to share literacy with their children in the language they know better and to continue to share literacy activities that are culturally relevant even though they do not resemble school activities. This feature keeps the program relevant to the populations involved in the program, regardless of language or culture (Auerbach, 1989). Then parents are introduced to new activities and practices that support literacy learning at school but which are still culturally and linguistically appropriate. As part of these programs, parents learn about schools and schools' expectations for their children. They also learn to appreciate their role as their children's first teachers and to value their participation and volunteering in school activities that support their children's learning.

Research and evaluation of these programs are based mostly on children's learning at home and changes in the home learning environments that support literacy learning for the whole family (Paratore, 2001; Rodríguez-Brown, 2004). Evidence of changes can be found in artifacts such as parents' self-reports, samples of parents' writing, or portfolios that parents prepare to share with teachers (Paratore). Some programs, such as Project FLAME, also collect data through case studies, standardized tests for both adults and children, and parent self-reporting on questionnaires (Rodríguez-Brown).

Originally, many of the programs directed toward culturally and linguistically different families and supported by a sociocultural view of family literacy were funded under Title I and Title VII ESEA of 1984. The programs were developed to enhance opportunities for literacy and biliteracy development and to improve relations between families and schools. Programs include The Boston English Family Literacy Program (Auerbach, 1992), The Intergenerational Literacy Program (Paratore, Melzi, & Krol-Sinclair, 1999), and Project FLAME (Rodríguez-Brown & Shanahan, 1989), among others.

A number of researchers support the enrichment perspective. Auerbach (1995) believed that family literacy programs should recognize parents' strengths, and any new knowledge regarding literacy learning should be built on what parents already know and do with their children at home. Goldenberg et al. (1992) agreed, stating that "intervention plans must be informed by parents' understandings no less than by our own, presumably more scientific ones" (p. 530). Delgado-Gaitan (1992) also believed that family literacy intervention programs should take into account the parents' views, start with parents' skills and knowledge, and then add to parents' literacy repertoire as appropriate. Because of the culturally different ways in which families share literacy, Heath (1983) suggested that schools should make accommodations to the types of literacy children practice at home rather than focus on the practices of middle-class, mainstream families.

In contrast with this opinion is Edwards' (1988, 1995) view that parents preferred to be shown directly strategies that they can use at home and that support success in reading for their children. Powell (1995), however, suggested that a middle ground can be achieved by providing parents with opportunities to participate in discussion groups focused on different issues. Through these discussions, rather than direct instruction, parents might change their beliefs and practices.

Family Literacy Models

Family literacy models have many variations in components, goals, and design. Below are some of the better known family literacy programs or models, listed according to their main features along with some of their characteristics.

Comprehensive (Integrated) Family Literacy Programs

These programs are called comprehensive because they integrate several components, one or two of which might be related to family literacy (learning at home). These models are widely used in programs supported by the U.S. Department of Education under Title I or under the Workforce Investment Partnership Act of 1998. Their components are more related to policy on welfare reform than to literacy per se (Darling, 1997). Their main objective is to prepare families for self-sufficiency and employment. In these programs, there is often no set curriculum, and instruction varies depending on time, teachers, and the population served.

The Kenan Trust Family Literacy Model

This model originated from the Parent and Child Education Program (PACE) initially developed and funded by the state of Kentucky in

1985. Subsequently this program model was supported through a grant from the William R. Kenan Jr. Charitable Trust in order to establish family literacy programs in Kentucky and North Carolina. The Kenan model (www.communityschools/handbook.pdf) led to the establishment of the National Family Literacy Center through a grant from the Kenan Foundation in 1989.

The original model included six components in support of children and families: early childhood education, adult education, parent time, parent-child together time (PACT), parents as volunteers, and career education. This family literacy model encourages the active role of parents as "first teachers."

The National Center for Family Literacy Model

Developed from the Kenan Model, this program (NCFL, 1995) integrates four components: adult education, children's education, parent and child together time (PACT), and parent time. The focus of the program is family self-sufficiency and school-to-work transitions. The model does not have a specific literacy-based design for "learning at home." Content in that area of literacy is to be included in PACT time and/or parent time. The model is directed toward low-income, at-risk families with low educational levels. Instruction for the PACT component varies depending on the population served and the quality and characteristics of personnel. Currently, the National Center for Family Literacy has demonstration programs funded by the Toyota Motor Corporation, the Bureau of Indian Affairs, the John S. and James L. Knight Foundation, and United Parcel Service, among others.

The Even Start Family Literacy Model

This program (www.ed.gov/admins/lead/account/nclbreference/page_pg7 .html) was originally authorized under Title I, Improving American Schools Act of 1988. Most recently the program was re-authorized by the Literacy Involves Families Together (LIFT) Act of 2000 (United States, 2000) and the No Child Left Behind Act of 2001 (United States, 2001). The National Center for Family Literacy (1995) model influenced the establishment of the Even Start Family Literacy Program, which was created to empower isolated, low-income, and academically at-risk families in order to (1) assist parents in becoming teachers of their children, (2) help children get ready for school and be successful in school programs, and (3) increase literacy skills for the whole family. The program includes components in adult education, parenting education, early childhood education, and interactive parent-child literacy activities. Even Start programs are required to design their program activities to use existing community resources, and activities must be intensive and of enough duration to make a difference in the participant families.

In this program, families learn literacy skills that allow them to be more productive in their personal, social, and occupational lives, through home-based instruction, center-based classes, and community-based enrichment activities. All Even Start programs are offered to families at no cost. Participant families may be generally described as having low education levels, limited resources, low self-esteem, and low literacy levels.

Models Developed and Used by Public Libraries

Viburnum/American Library Association Rural Family Literacy Project

This literacy project was established in 1992 in Louisiana with a grant from the Viburnum Foundation (www.tsl.state.tx.us/pubs/obe/virburnum.html). The project uses the resources of public libraries to create partnerships in support of parenting and family stability and to improve family reading skills. There is not a specific design underlying the planning of family literacy activities. In some areas, the project has resulted in the creation of multimedia literacy rooms and summer reading programs that include parents.

Beginning With Books

This nationally recognized family literacy program (beginningwith books.org) was founded in 1984 and is affiliated with The Carnegie Library of Pittsburgh. It promotes family literacy through a variety of programs including The Gift Book Program, Read Together, Read-Aloud Parent Clubs, and Project Beacon. In The Gift Book Program, low-income parents of young children receive quality paperbacks through agencies including Head Start programs, drug and child-abuse agencies, food banks, homeless shelters, and well-baby clinics. Parents are encouraged to read to their children every day and are invited to visit the library for other free books. This program reaches over 6,000 families a year.

The Read Together project recruits volunteers to read one-on-one to children and to supervise other creative activities while parents receive literacy tutoring from the Greater Pittsburgh Literacy Council. Parents also learn about reading to their children. Children receive three gift books during the year, and both parents and children are assisted in library usage.

The goals of the Read-Aloud Parent Club program are: (1) to help parents become more skillful and confident in reading to their children; (2) to encourage daily reading aloud and regular library visits; and (3) to stimulate children's literacy development through family literacy. Parents meet weekly, receive free books, and are invited to obtain library cards and borrow books. Childcare is provided in some cases and meetings end with parent/child time. Clubs have been established for Head Start parents, residents of public housing, and kindergarten Title I parents.

Project Beacon is an outreach program which provides children's books and in-service training on emergent literacy to family day-care homes, day-care centers, and parents in low-income neighborhoods.

Parenting and Adult Education Programs

These programs are specifically focused on parent training, but the training is geared more toward child development and only indirectly toward literacy.

Parents as Teachers (PAT)

PAT (Parents as Teachers National Center, n.d.), described as an early childhood parent education and family support program, was developed in 1981. This national, integrated services program is available to all families regardless of their socioeconomic level. The purpose of the program is to enhance child development and school achievement through parent education.

PAT has an established curriculum and certifies parent educators to work with parents. The program's main goals are to increase parents' knowledge about early childhood development in order to improve practice, to increase children's school readiness and school success, to provide early detection of developmental problems and/or health issues with families, and to prevent child abuse and neglect. According to the developers, the PAT program "blends" with other programs, and it is used as a component of Even Start, Early Head Start, and Healthy Families America.

The Home Instruction Program for Preschool Youngsters (HIPPY)

HIPPY was originally developed in Israel in 1968 and first implemented in the United States in 1984. It is a two-year, home-based, early childhood education intervention program directed toward parents with limited education. The program supports parents as they prepare their children for school. It is expected that children from program participants will do better in cognitive skills, adaptation to the class-room, and school achievement than children whose parents do not participate in the program (Baker, Piotrkowski, & Brooks-Gunn, 1998).

The Bowdoin Method

The Bowdoin Method is a "program to empower families with the basic skills and confidence to meet social, emotional and academic needs of their children" (Bowdoin Method, n.d., p. 1). The program is based on the belief that children who enter school with good language and pre-reading skills will read well and succeed in school in later years. This model, validated by the U.S. Department of Education, includes four basic curricula entitled: Your Baby and You, Bowdoin Method I—English, Bowdoin Method I—Spanish, and Bowdoin Method II. The curricula comprise a variety of workshops which include issues of self-esteem, emotional and behavioral development, as well as readiness and reading skills. The program is described as multicultural and intended for low-literacy parents to help them become their child's first and best teachers.

New York Parents Initiative

In 1989, family education and family literacy programs were developed and implemented across New York to provide parent literacy and adult education, developmental early childhood education, parent education and support, and intergenerational (parent/child) activities. The programs were developed and implemented by staff of the state's Adult Centers for Comprehensive Education and Support Services (ACCESS) and the Center for Family Resources (CFR) in Mineola, New York.

Five of these programs then became sites of the New York Parents Initiative (www.cnycf.org/news/index.cfm?id=128). Staff members from each site were trained in parenting education in order to develop their own family education programming. Although each site developed a slightly different program to support parents, the programs share a philosophy that is based on family support principles. Some sites have created parent resource centers, while others offer parent support groups, parent-child activity groups, and computer classes for parents and children together. Each program has built upon its own resources and strengths, but all sites encourage participants to set and achieve goals for themselves and their families.

Family Literacy Programs Based on Research in Literacy Learning

The purpose of these programs is to teach parents ways in which they can support their children's learning. The design of each program is informed by research on emergent literacy and literacy learning at home. Some programs include parents and children together in the activities while others provide services only to parents, but positive outcomes are expected and measured from both parents and children.

The Intergenerational Literacy Project (ILP)

This program model was developed in 1989 by Paratore (2001). The goal of the program is to support adult participants in learning to read and write in English and in using storybook reading activities to enhance their children's literacy development. The program was designed with the understanding that literacy is a sociocultural process. Bilingualism and biculturalism are seen as positive influences which expand the possibilities for new learning and cognitive development. Participants' first languages and cultures are respected, are a central part of program activities, and are used to help participants connect with new information.

Data collected for evaluation and research purposes show participants' improvement in both reading and writing. Self-reports on the practice of shared readings at home indicate that parents use the procedure as a new tool in support of their children's learning at home.

Project FLAME (Family Literacy: Aprendiendo, Mejorando, Educando [Learning, Improving, Educating])

Based on the concept of family literacy as part of learning at home, this program was developed at the University of Illinois at Chicago in 1989 in response to a need for family literacy models for culturally and linguistically different families (Rodríguez-Brown & Shanahan, 1989). The original program was supported by the U.S. Department of Education under Title VII ESEA. Subsequently, the program was validated as an Academic Excellence Program by the state of Illinois in 1995, and since then has been adopted by more than 50 sites nationwide.

The family literacy component of the program (Parents as Teachers) is based on what research says about literacy opportunity, literacy modeling, literacy interactions, and the need for a home-school connection. Central to the program design is respect for parents' knowledge and language in the planning of literacy activities. Parents' knowledge and ways of learning are used as steppingstones to new literacy learning activities and an expanded parental repertoire of literacy activities.

The Parents as Learners component includes classes in English as a Second Language (ESL), General Education Development (GED), or Basic Skills. This component was created to provide opportunities for parents to become models of learning for their children. It also serves as an enticement for parents to attend program activities. This model is discussed in detail later in the book.

Summary of Family Literacy and Current Program Models

These descriptions of some of the programs using the term family literacy emphasize the fact that program models have different interpretations or definitions for the meaning of family literacy. Based on their definition, most programs fall into one of the following two categories.

Broad Definitions

Some programs are based on broad definitions of family literacy, are designed to fit current funding policy requirements, and are specifically created to be components of "integrated" or "comprehensive" models. Programs such as Even Start are geared toward low-income families and academically at-risk children. They are comprehensive in the sense that they offer integrated services to both parents and children. These program models are designed in response to the requirements for U.S. Department of Education funding under Even Start and the Workforce Act of 1998. An important goal for the programs is to support and move parents toward economic self-sufficiency and the work force and, as such, the parent-child and parenting sessions are not at the center of the program activities. However, in practice, they do seem to focus a lot of attention on parenting skills and directed parent-child times.

In terms of benefits to children's literacy, there are a number of disadvantages to these models. First, they do not offer a basic design for literacy activities that can be used across programs. If each site is required to develop its own program and curriculum, the content for the components might, and often does, vary from program to program, depending on the developers' philosophy of how to deal with "at-risk" families. Second, these programs are based on a "deficit" model, which, during the planning of activities, does not take into account the knowledge and strengths of the involved families and what they might contribute to the learning situations.

Third, these programs lack a theoretical framework to identify what is important in terms of family literacy programs and/or adult education designs. Although the components for the models are listed, each site might choose different activities to fulfill the requirement for a component. This results in little consistency across sites. The integration of services between components is not always evident.

Fourth, cultural relevance is not considered, even when the programs are designed to serve culturally and linguistically different populations. Program design and implementation does not recognize or value the languages and cultures of program participants.

Finally, results of the programs are expressed in terms of duration and intensity of services. Can a program be considered effective if the services offered are not relevant for the populations it serves, even if the program is of sufficient duration and intensity? In a diverse society, the issue of cultural relevance cannot be overlooked when discussing program quality.

Narrow Definitions

The second category of program models defines literacy from a narrow perspective that relies on specific research in early literacy learning (e.g., Paratore, 2001; Rodríguez-Brown, 2004). Most are currently funded by school districts, foundations, or corporations, and are not required to meet specific government funding criteria. Their purpose is more often the development of literacy skills in the home to support the children's literacy in school. However, not all programs cover the same topics. Project FLAME (Rodríguez-Brown & Shanahan, 1989) is called a comprehensive family literacy model because it covers reading, writing, and oral language activities, in contrast to models that deal only with a specific activity, such as shared book readings.

There are a number of advantages for literacy development with models that are based on a narrow definition of family literacy. First, their instructional design is supported by a theoretical framework based on research in literacy learning at home, parental involvement, and children's achievement. The activities of the program usually deal with specific aspects of emergent literacy, which might be new or different for the parents. Second, following the enrichment model, these programs usually recognize and use the knowledge that adults bring into the program. Even though the programs might be targeted toward low-literacy and low-education families, there is not an expectation that all parents in the program are illiterate. Since parents usually want to support their children's success in school, the programs teach parents new practices for early literacy learning that they can share with their children. They also encourage parents to add the new practices to their existing literacy repertoire. The expectation is that parents will support literacy learning at home in ways that are culturally and linguistically relevant, but that also support children's school learning.

Third, the design of the programs and the influence of research findings require that they be sensitive to cultural and linguistic differences in the families. Parents are encouraged to participate in the planning of activities for the program. Fourth, there is more often a basic design that is used at all sites. Project FLAME (Rodríguez-Brown & Shanahan, 1989), for example, has been replicated at numerous sites nationwide. Replicability is a characteristic that allows comparison across programs using a particular model. This advantage is lacking in many family literacy models, and it has implications in terms of accountability and program effectiveness studies.

Finally, evaluation of a narrow definition model is more closely related to literacy outcomes. Beyond information on attendance, retention rates, duration, and intensity of program services, program evaluations also focus on participants' self-reports and observations of literacy uses at home, changes in attitudes toward and uses of literacy, and home-school relations. Program effectiveness also should reflect how different program models use the strengths of their participants in support of learning (Gladsden, 1994; Rodríguez-Brown & Shanahan, 1989).

Personal Reflections on Current Models

I believe that parents who are effective teachers engage their children in activities that are culturally relevant to them and also support the children's cognitive development and readiness for schooling. As a result, I find myself in conflict with those models that describe family literacy as a school-to-work program, or a program that leads to self-sufficiency. In my experience working with parents, I have observed an interesting side effect of an enrichment program model. Even when the focus of the program is literacy, the program enhances a sense of self-esteem and self-efficacy in participants. This in turn leads them to volunteer to work at school or to seek employment. The difference is that self-sufficiency and employment are not the main objectives of the program.

Also, because of my work with parents who are learning English as a second language, it is very hard for me to disregard the fact that many participants in family literacy programs who are learning English might already be literate in their first language. They understand the processes of reading and writing. It is incorrect to describe them as illiterate when what they need is to learn English.

I believe that parents support their children's literacy learning better when they use the language they know better. When they use their native language, and the one in which they are literate, parents are more fluent readers, they can ask better questions, extend the stories they read, and write better stories with their children (Mulhern, 1991). Through all these activities, parents support not only literacy learning, but also cognitive development and preparation for school. Why teach parents to practice literacy with their children in a language they don't know well, when they can do much better if they use their first language?

Another question to be raised is why we must combine programs that support parents and children working together in literacy activities with programs that prepare parents to get jobs, even though the program is described as a family literacy program. Although both activities are commendable, I question the tendency to keep them together when the objectives of the activities are so different. If the programs are called family literacy, they should focus on literacy, and they should cover oral language as well as reading and writing. According to Heath (1983), reading, writing, and storytelling should be encouraged in family literacy. Programs need to include not only skills-based instruction in reading and writing but also oral language activities within a cultural way of learning that is relevant to the participants' families.

Another practice that I take issue with is the requirement that parents share literacy activities with their children in a school-like manner. In this regard, I believe that in a diverse society, it is important that parents use their cultural ways of teaching to support their children's learning. I am not saying that parents should not learn to teach their children in ways that are similar to those used at school. It is important for parents to visit classrooms and learn about how teachers teach. However, culturally diverse parents should be offered the opportunity to add to their teaching repertoire as part of their participation in family literacy programs, rather than trying to replace their existing literacy practices.

Another issue is whether programs should provide direct services to parents or to parents and children. To me, either of those modalities should be fine, but accountability should examine the effect of the program on the children from participant families. There is also the issue of defining the word "intergenerational" as part of a program description. Some programs that serve parents call themselves intergenerational because parents practice what they learn during program sessions with their children at home. Others are called intergenerational because parents and children are part of all program activities and parents practice with their children as part of the literacy activities of the program.

I also want to raise the issue of whether family literacy is a field of study with its own research-based framework, only a component of parental involvement (learning at home), or a concept created to fit current policy and political agendas. From my perspective, there is enough research and varied theoretical frameworks to sustain family literacy as a field of research. This is also an open field to research the impact of learning at home, the effects of home-school connections, and the impact of multiple cultural ways of learning and discourses on children's literacy learning and preparation for school. Of course, there is also a need for research on policy and the effects of different literacy practices on children and their families.

Finally, program models should reflect the original purpose of family literacy. The focus should be on the child and on ways that parents can support literacy learning at home or in the community. Teachers and schools need to be aware of research on learning at home, including the differences in cultural ways of learning and discourses that children bring to school in a diverse society. This way, teachers would be able to recognize and respect differences and facilitate the home-school connection. Parents should be recognized as their children's first teachers. They want to be respected and welcomed at the school and also provided with information and training on how learning takes place in school. Family literacy should be a two-way street where homes and schools support each other in providing children with opportunities to learn and succeed in school and in life, no matter what their differences in culture and/or language.

Part II

Project FLAME

Part II takes an in-depth look at one model of family literacy, Project FLAME, which has been successful with Latino parents. It includes a detailed description of the program, its sociocultural framework, and a number of analyses of data collected from participants. Personal reflections of parents and program personnel are also provided. Finally, there is also a discussion of ways in which Project FLAME has adjusted to the needs of its constituents, becoming more effective by becoming more relevant.

After explaining the cultural context for FLAME in the Latino community, Chapter 3 describes the model and its various components and modules, including aspects of its evolution since it was developed in 1989. The research and theory leading to the development of a sociocultural framework for the model is described in Chapter 4. This framework and its principles guide all program activities.

Chapter 5 addresses the effectiveness of Project FLAME using both quantitative and qualitative data collected from parents and their children over a period of six years. Although the program is directed toward parents of children between three and nine years old, the children's literacy learning is supported by what parents learn in program activities.

Chapter 6 relates lessons learned from the experiences of working with families in the Latino community. This includes cultural practices and attitudes of the parents in the community, as well as program planning and implementation, especially with culturally and linguistically diverse groups.

Chapter 3

The Home–School Connection

Cultural Context for Project FLAME

As their young children's first teachers, parents play a vital role in their children's lives and in their preparation for formal schooling. It is important that schools view parents, the home, and community as resources in support of children's transition to and success in the school setting. This is especially relevant in schools with large populations of culturally and linguistically diverse children, who are the focus of this book.

Parents should feel that the ways they encourage, teach, and share knowledge with their children at home and their efforts to support what their children learn at school are valuable, and that these ways of learning at home are recognized as such by the school. In order for that to happen, parents need to feel welcomed, respected, important, and validated by the school and teachers.

To understand issues related to parents' involvement in their children's early literacy learning, the following questions need to be addressed in schools with diverse populations since parents have the potential to become resources in supporting the role of the schools in educating all children. Why is it important for parents to partner with teachers in support of children's learning? How might parents support their children as they transition from home to school? Why is it important for today's schools to see parents as resources? Do schools need to rethink the ways in which they reach out to families? Why is this important today more than ever? The following pages discuss these questions.

Demographic Changes and Schooling

During the last 20 years, school populations in the United States have become more diverse, not only in terms of race, but also ethnicity, language, and culture. According to the U.S. Census Bureau (Larsen,

2004), this diversity is not confined to urban areas but exists almost everywhere. Demographics about the population are reported in terms used by the Census Bureau. When determining origins, the Bureau uses the term native population to indicate those who were born in the United States or its territories, or were born abroad of parents who were U.S. citizens. The term foreign-born refers to those individuals who were not U.S. citizens at birth. Hispanic is used to indicate all Spanish-speaking individuals.

Information from the U.S. Census Bureau shows that in 2003 foreign-born individuals accounted for 11.7% of the total population. This included 53.3% from Latin America, 25% from Asia, 13.7% from Europe, and the remaining 8% from other areas of the world (Larsen, 2004). These individuals live all over the United States: 36.5% in the West, 29.2% in the South, 22% in the Northeast and 11.3% in the Midwest. About two-fifths (44.4%) of these immigrants live in central cities in metropolitan areas, 50.3% live outside central cities but within metropolitan areas, and only 5.3% live in non-metropolitan areas.

Age

In 2003, individuals aged 25–44 comprised 45.1% of the foreign-born population in comparison with 27% of the native population within the same age range. Only 8.9% of foreign-born individuals were less than 18 years old in comparison to 27.8% of natives. The number of foreign-born at this age level is small because most of the children of foreign-born parents were born in the United States and as such they are considered natives.

Education

Immigrants aged 25 and over are less likely to have graduated from high school (67.2%) than natives (87.5%). The highest percentage of high school graduates among foreign-born individuals comes from Asia (87%), Europe (84.9%), and other regions (83.5%). This is in sharp contrast to those from Latin America where only 49.1% have graduated from high school (Sable & Stennett, 1998).

Occupation

More foreign-born workers are in service occupations (23.3%) in comparison to native workers (14.9%), who are more likely to be in professional or management specialty occupations (36.2%) in comparison to foreign-born workers (26.9%). Among the foreign-born, people from

Asia are more often in managerial and professional jobs (47%) in comparison to Latin Americans (12.7%). These facts indicate lower incomes and a higher level of poverty (16.6%) among the foreign-born population when compared with natives (11.5%).

Language

The U.S. 2000 Census (Ramirez & de la Cruz, 2003) revealed that 18% of the total population aged five and over (47 million people) speak a language other than English. This is an increase of 4% from the previous census in 1990. Of those who report the use of a language other than English at home, 55% feel they speak English very well.

Spanish is the non-English language most commonly used at home. Spanish speakers grew by about 60% between 1990 and 2000. After English and Spanish, Chinese is the most commonly spoken language at home, followed by French and German. Chinese jumped from fifth to second during the same period of time.

The West is the geographic area of the United States with the largest number and proportion of non-English speakers. Spanish is the language spoken more than any other language group in all regions of the United States.

Hispanic Demographics

The demographics for the Hispanic population are different from the other cultural groups. According to the 2000 census, the Hispanic population in the United States increased by more than 50% from 1990 (Guzman, 2001). More than three-quarters of the Hispanic population lives in the West and the South (half of them in California and Texas). Hispanics are also present in some non-traditional counties in North Carolina, Georgia, Iowa, Arkansas, Minnesota, and Nevada.

The Hispanic population is younger than the U.S. population—35% of Hispanics were less than 18 years old in 2000 compared to 25.7% of the U.S. native population. Two of five Hispanics are foreign-born, and Hispanic households tend to be larger than those of non-Hispanic whites.

Census data show that Hispanics are more likely than non-Hispanic whites to live in central cities in metropolitan areas (Fields & Casper, 2001). In terms of education, only 57% of Hispanics 25 years old or older have graduated from high school in comparison with the rate for non-Hispanic whites (88.7%).

The above statistics illustrate how today's schools are more diverse than ever, and issues of diversity, including language and culture, have to be dealt with in classrooms everyday. This issue seems more critical with the Hispanic population because it is the fastest growing immigrant group.

Diversity and Parents' Role in Their Children's Learning

To effectively address diversity in order to educate ALL children, schools and teachers must become aware of parents' differing cultures and views about their role in their children's education. Parents who are from other countries might have different expectations about schools, or they might not be aware of the culture of schools in the United States. Due to language and cultural differences, immigrant parents often feel very little connection to the schools in their community, and they do not know what is expected of them. They might feel frustrated about not knowing what to do, but they are afraid to ask.

In many cultures, teachers and schools are held in high regard. Teachers are seen as more knowledgeable about and capable of educating children. Parents might be unaware of the need to interact with teachers and schools as part of their children's education. Parents also might be shy or hesitant to talk to teachers or ask for information because they feel it is not correct to interfere with the teacher or the school. Who are they to tell the teacher that their child already knows something, or to ask for an explanation about rules for homework?

Hidalgo, Bright, Siu, Swap, and Epstein (1995) believe that schools unwittingly punish parents for not contributing to their children's learning in a prescribed way. It is important for schools to reach out to diverse families and learn about differences between the ways children learn at home and the ways they learn at school. It is also important for schools to share with parents knowledge about the school culture and teacher expectations for their children. Schools must provide opportunities for parents to add to their knowledge about teaching and learning by offering programs that teach them new ways to support their children's learning both at home and at school. Such programs are more effective when schools use parents as resources and when parents feel they can contribute significantly to their children's learning.

Latino Parents and Schooling

Within Latino families, lack of English proficiency and low levels of schooling are reasons parents give for not being able to support their children's literacy learning. Also, Latino parents view teachers as experts and do not feel parents should interfere with what they consider the teacher's role (Flores, Cousin, & Diaz, 1991). New immigrant parents see their role as teachers differently from the mainstream population, as reflected in their use of different words for education. In Spanish there are two words to indicate teaching, *educar* (to educate) and *enseñar* (to teach), with very distinct and specific meanings. In general, Latino parents feel that their role is one of *educar* (educating) their children. That is, their role is to support their children in becoming good people. They do this by teaching morals, manners, and values. In contrast, they believe that the school's role is that of *enseñar* (teaching) which means teaching math, science, reading, writing, and other academic subjects. This distinction or dichotomy has been found and discussed previously by different researchers (Goldenberg, 1987; Reese, Balzano et al., 1995; Rodríguez-Brown, 2001b; Valdes, 1996).

Parents' ambivalence about their role as teachers and their *respeto*, or respect (Valdes, 1996) and high regard for teachers as experts make parents question whether the teachers expect, or even want, them to support their children's learning at home. Teachers can easily clarify this issue by explicitly stating their expectations for Latino parents' involvement in their children's learning. Reese and Gallimore (2000) found that parents responded positively to explicit requests to help their children. The researchers believe that although Latino parents' goals and beliefs are influenced by traditional values, they are willing to adapt to the expectations of the American schools. They recommend that teachers make explicit demands of Latino parents for reading at home as a regular part of homework. This activity will promote desired behaviors and in the process allow parents to acquire a different view of literacy development. Reese and Gallimore also recommend that school districts consider long-term family literacy programs, which allow parents to be participants in program activities at the same time that they become literacy leaders in schools and communities where they live.

Research with Latino families has shown that parents have high expectations for their children, but they are not sure how they can help or foster school success (Delgado-Gaitan, 1992; Goldenberg & Gallimore, 1991). Reese and Gallimore (2000) found that Latino families are willing to learn and use new ways to share literacy with their children, as long as the new cultural ways of learning do not conflict with their values and morals. In Latino families, the concept of "familia" (family) is very important in their daily life (Abi-Nader, 1991). Many activities involve family members, and decisions are made for the good of the family rather than the individual. This concept also increases parents' motivation to participate in family literacy activities that benefit not only themselves but also their children. To this effect, parents might be more willing to participate in a program where they learn things that can benefit them as parents, but that could also have a direct affect on their children's learning and schooling.

cultural differences within "Latino community"?

Family Literacy Programs

In order to meet the needs of culturally diverse parents and families, family literacy programs should be designed to use the parents' language and knowledge as resources for learning new ways to support their children's learning. Such programs are ideal for schools to validate the parents' roles as teachers and to socialize parents to the culture and expectations of the schools their children attend. Programs also should acknowledge a broad range of culturally different ways of knowing and learning, and provide access to and comfort in dealing with schools. According to Shanahan, Mulhern, and Rodríguez-Brown (1995), through family literacy programs, children and adults in a family can find simultaneous and connected opportunities to share knowledge and learn. In new immigrant communities, these programs also help to reduce isolation from schools and allow parents to extend their repertoire of activities to support their children's learning at school.

Family literacy programs for culturally and linguistically different parents should address parents' personal goals, value families' knowledge and language, regard families as resources, and provide parents with access to information and resources that encourage children's success. Program activities should build on existing home literacy practices rather than expect parents to abandon their culturally relevant ways and adopt mainstream literacy practices, which foster a school-like transfer of skills or knowledge from parent to child (Ada, 1988; Auerbach, 1989; Paratore, 2001; Quintero & Huerta-Macias, 1990a; Rodríguez-Brown, 2004). For Latino families, family literacy programs are a more culturally relevant way to support parents' literacy skills than adult education programs that are designed to teach English, basic skills, or job skills and where parents feel that they are doing something only for themselves and not for their children (Rodríguez-Brown & Meehan, 1998).

The concepts discussed above are central to the planning and design of programs directed toward the Latino population. The following pages describe Project FLAME (Family Literacy: Aprendiendo, Mejorando, Educando [Learning, Improving, Educating]), a family literacy model developed originally to serve Latino families (Rodríguez-Brown & Shanahan, 1989). The program serves as context for the discussion of the home–school connection that is central to this book.

Project FLAME

Project FLAME (Rodríguez-Brown & Shanahan, 1989) was developed in response to the need for Latino parents to get more involved in their children's learning at home, and the need to reduce discontinuities between home and school. In creating an acronym for the program, we decided to include words in both Spanish and English to represent the value we place on bilingualism. FLAME is considered a comprehensive family literacy model because it includes activities that deal not only with literacy but also with the home–school connection by providing activities that allow parents and teachers to talk and work together in order to facilitate the children's transition between home and school. The program is intended for Latino families who have children between the ages of three and nine.

The original FLAME program was part of a proposal for funding from the U.S. Department of Education (Rodríguez-Brown & Shanahan). The purpose of the program was to enhance the literacy learning opportunities of a mostly Latino, new immigrant population. Several beliefs about literacy learning guided the development of the program:

- Literacy learning is a more culturally bound activity than other aspects of school learning, and, as such, it is more influenced by parental and home factors.
- The literacy culture of the home is more likely to diverge from the literacy culture of the school when children come from homes where English is a second language, or where English is not used at all.
- Communication styles, views of literacy, and the nature of literacy interactions at home differ from those at school and this difference has an impact on Latino children's literacy development.

More recent research by Gee (1999), The New London Group (1996), Goldenberg (1989), Reese and Gallimore (2000), and Rogers (2002) adds support to these beliefs.

FLAME uses the family as the context for program activities, since the concept of "familia" (Abi-Nader, 1991) is central to cultural descriptions of Latinos. More specifically, meeting the needs of the family is one of the greatest motivations for Latino parents to support their children's learning and school success (Delgado-Gaitan, 1992; Quintero & Huerta-Macias, 1990b). Therefore, family literacy is the vehicle used to increase opportunities for families to learn new ways to support their children's literacy learning in order to reduce the discontinuities between home and school. Based on these beliefs about literacy development and Latino family cultural preferences, the program seeks to train parents to become good literacy models and to support the literacy development of their children in the language they know better.

Project FLAME is a community program, based in the public schools and delivered by the University of Illinois at Chicago. With funding from the Department of Education, the program was first implemented in three public schools in Chicago in 1989. It served approximately 20 families per school during the first three years. Since then, it has expanded to serve parents in 14 schools, and has served around 200 families annually. Currently, and with different funding, the program is offered at two Chicago public schools and two Chicago park district facilities which serve multiple schools. Also, the program model has been disseminated nationally to about 54 sites, which have adopted the FLAME model as part of their family literacy training program.

Program Assumptions and Theoretical Design

The design of Project FLAME is based on four assumptions about parents and literacy development:

- A supportive home environment is essential to literacy development.
- Parents can have a positive effect on their children's learning.
- Parents who are confident and successful learners themselves will be the most effective teachers for their children.
- Literacy is the school subject most likely to be influenced by the social and cultural contexts of the family.

These assumptions have resulted in the creation of four specific objectives for the program. These objectives are:

1   To increase the parents' ability to provide literacy opportunities for their children.
2   To increase parents' ability to act as positive literacy models for their children.
3   To improve parents' literacy skills so they can more efficiently initiate, encourage, support, and extend their children's learning.
4   To increase and improve the relationship between parents and the schools.

In order to meet these objectives, the program design includes four components that are supported by research in literacy learning: literacy opportunity, literacy modeling, literacy interaction, and home–school connection.

Literacy Opportunity

In order to perform well in school literacy learning, children need to be familiar with a culture of literacy, see literacy in action, and have opportunities to practice and experiment with literacy. A supportive home environment and the availability of literacy materials at home can provide children with these opportunities. According to Wheeler (1971), the provision of such opportunities alone has been found to be a powerful stimulus to literacy learning in young children.

Opportunities for language play, singing, and rhyming are important for raising children's phonemic awareness, or the awareness of sounds in their language (Baker, Serpell, & Sonnenschein, 1995). According to Teale and Sulzby (1986), the development of phonemic awareness is important for later reading achievement. Reese, Garnier, Gallimore, and Goldenberg (2000) found that Spanish-speaking children who had emergent literacy skills in their native language transitioned quickly into English reading and showed a higher level of reading achievement even when they reached middle school. This suggests a need to encourage parents to provide opportunities for literacy learning and oral language at home in their native language.

Project FLAME teaches parents how to locate and select appropriate books, magazines, and other literacy materials for their children. Moreover, parents learn to use public libraries to increase the availability of literacy materials appropriate for their children at home. Parents develop a literacy center at home where young children can use items such as pencils, paper, markers, scissors, books, and other materials in support of their early literacy learning; older children can read books and do homework.

Literacy Modeling

For the purposes of the program, a literacy model is defined as a significant person in the child's environment who uses literacy in an open and obvious manner. Modeling is important since children who see their parents reading and writing at home are usually better readers (MetriTech, 1987). Furthermore, several studies report that efforts to change the mothers' strategies for reading to their children have been successful in improving literacy learning for both Latino children (Gallimore & Goldenberg, 1989) and other low SES children (Edwards, 1988). However, Gallimore and Goldenberg (1989) found that Latino parents who are just learning English tended not to share literacy with their children. This could be due to parents' limited literacy skills or their lack of proficiency in English. Also, Heath (1986) found that parents, in their zeal to expose their children to English, sometimes failed to provide a rich, active language environment at home. Several studies have shown that parents were more likely to serve as good literacy models and to participate in their children's literacy learning when they saw themselves as effective learners (Nickse, Speicher, & Bucheck, 1988; Van Fossen & Sticht, 1991).

In FLAME, the primary vehicle for helping parents become positive literacy models is ESL and/or basic skills classes offered through the program. Parents are encouraged to increase their own literacy and language use, to use reading and writing in the company of children, and to draw their children's attention to subtle uses of reading and writing.

Literacy Interaction

This component is well supported by research. Direct interaction between parents and children has a positive influence on children's learning (Paratore, 1994; Paratore et al., 1999; Tobin, 1981). For example, children who are read to often are more successful at school than those who do not have such experiences (Feiltelson & Goldstein, 1986). These types of activities acquaint children with story structures and literacy conventions (Teale, 1984). Literacy interactions can include formal direct instruction, as well as activities such as reading to children or encouraging them to pretend read.

Through Project FLAME, parents participate in activities that prepare them for reading more effectively to their children. They learn how to talk with their children about books. In addition, parents learn the value of songs, games, and other interactive activities that support their children's phonemic awareness. They also learn about community resources that they can share with their children as a way to support their children's literacy learning.

Home–School Connection

According to Goldenberg (1987), Latino children's literacy knowledge was highest in situations in which teachers and parents maintained frequent contact with each other. Also, Silvern (1988) found that social and cultural discontinuities between the home and the school interfered with literacy learning. Successful home–school connections can minimize these discontinuities. Parents who feel more comfortable talking to teachers might be more receptive to schools' requests on behalf of their children's education. When parents see that schools value what they know, they will feel more confident about their abilities to support their children's learning at home. The home–school connection component of Project FLAME addresses the need for parents to understand what happens in classrooms, and what the school's expectations are for their children. Conversely, teachers also need to learn about parents' concerns and aspirations.

Through Project FLAME, parents learn about the role of teachers in their children's education. Classroom visits are organized for parents to observe teachers. This activity helps parents establish early communication with teachers and practice discussing literacy learning. The visits also increase home–school collaboration with their children's teachers. Through these classroom visits and informal talks with teachers, good relations and mutual respect develop between parents and schools.

Instructional Program

The instructional design of the program includes two modules, or integrated sets of activities, Parents as Teachers, and Parents as Learners. Although the theoretical design for FLAME has four components, they are not taught separately. Rather, program activities are planned so that each one can contribute to more than one objective or component of the design. This approach is an effort to deal with the complexity of creating a home literacy culture which reflects the parents' cultural ways and also supports and connects with ways in which their children learn at school. The program activities recognize and reflect these subtle intricacies.

Parents as Teachers

The Parents as Teachers module comprises what is actually the family literacy program. It consists of bimonthly workshops with a focus on the four objectives for home literacy, as described in the theoretical design of the program. Sessions are conducted in the language that parents know better. They focus on literacy opportunity (increasing the range of literacy materials and experiences available at home); literacy modeling (encouraging parents to model literacy uses to their children); literacy interaction (demonstrating ways to engage in literacy activities with children); and the home–school connection (providing opportunities for teacher-parent discussions and classroom observation). Table 3.1 lists the topics of the workshops and describes the contents of each.

Workshops are organized around a common parallel structure which usually includes the following components:

a. An Introductory Activity
   This includes an introduction to the topic and questions for brainstorming so that parents bring up what they know about the topic and what is relevant to them. If parents do not offer enough input, they are provided with prompts which allow them to connect with the topic.

b. Discussion
   Questions are raised that allow parents to talk about the topic in more detail. Usually questions are provided, but parents are also encouraged to bring their own questions into the discussion. The

Table 3.1 Project FLAME—Parents as Teachers Sessions

Creating Home Literacy Centers
This session demonstrates creating and using a home literacy activity center in a box that includes pencils, crayons, paper, scissors, paste, magazines, pictures, etc.

Book Sharing
This session discusses and demonstrates the most effective ways to share books with children. Parents discuss how to talk about books and share books when their own literacy is limited.

Book Selection
This session highlights criteria for selecting quality books appropriate for children's needs and interests.

Library Visit
This session includes a public library tour, complete with applications for library cards.

Book Fair
In this session, parents purchase (with coupons provided by the program) English or Spanish language books for their children.

Teaching the ABCs
This session explores simple ways to teach letters and sounds, with an emphasis on language games, songs, and language experience activities.

Children's Writing
This session explores how young children write and demonstrates ways to encourage writing at home.

Community Literacy
This session highlights ways parents can share their own literacy uses with their children while at the market, in the community, and during other daily activities outside the home and at home.

Classroom Observations
In this session, parents visit classrooms to gain a sense of how their children are taught in schools.

Parent-Teacher Get-Togethers
In this session, parents, teachers, and principals gather for a guided discussion about children's education.

Math at Home
This session demonstrates games and activities for helping children understand numbers and arithmetic.

Parents and Homework
This session discusses and demonstrates ways in which parents can monitor and help with children's homework even when they cannot do the homework themselves.

Songs, Games, and Language: A Family Celebration
This lesson serves as the culminating event for the Project FLAME Literacy Curriculum. The lesson is designed as an event that the entire family can attend.

questions might lead parents to develop categories or more specific topics to cover. Parents usually participate actively in this discussion.

c.. Role-Playing

Participants usually present ideas about how they work with their children at home on issues related to the topic of the workshop. Usually they develop role-playing activities that lead to a discussion about various approaches to teaching or supporting children's learning in ways that are congruent with the home discourse patterns and the parents' cultural ways of teaching and learning.

d. Wrapping Up the Session

During this time parents discuss what they have learned in the workshop and ways in which they plan to support their children's learning at home using what they have learned. To support the parents' discussions, sessions usually start with one or two pre-planned questions and then parents are asked to offer their own questions for discussion. In all these discussions there is an opportunity for participants to bring new questions and concerns to the attention of the group.

e. Follow-Up and Homework

Parents are asked to practice what they have learned with their children at home. They are asked to keep notes or just try to remember what happens with their children and to be ready to discuss their experience and ask more questions before the next workshop.

This format is used by parent trainers and the university staff to plan the actual lesson specific to their site. See Appendix A for a sample of a typical FLAME lesson.

Through participation in various activities of the program, parents are expected to learn:

- how to create a home literacy center;
- how to select children's books that are appropriate and enjoyable;
- how to share books with children and talk about books when their own literacy is limited;
- how to use library resources;
- how to teach the ABCs through language games, songs, and language experience activities;
- how to encourage young children to write at home;
- how to find literacy uses with their children while at home, at the market, and during other daily activities in the community;
- how their children are taught in schools through classroom observations;
- how to discuss their children's education with teachers and principals;

- how to help their children understand numbers and arithmetic through games and activities;
- how to monitor and help with their children's homework even when they do not know the subject areas themselves.

To make the activities relevant for the intended population, Project FLAME involved parents in the planning of the workshops. Also, cultural ways and discourses used in their homes also incorporated into the activities as parents learned about more specific ways to support the home–school connection.

Parents as Learners

The Parents as Learners module includes instruction in basic skills, GED, or ESL, according to the needs of the project participants. Sessions take place twice a week for two hours. The purpose of the module is to support the role of parents as learners and as models of literacy learning. Actually, these classes have also served as a hook or recruitment tool to attract parents to the program.

The twice-weekly Parents as Learners sessions are chosen based on the specific literacy learning needs of the parents at a particular site. For ESL instruction, FLAME uses a communicative competence perspective and a participatory approach, which is based on ideas from Auerbach (1989). First, parents choose the topics for the lessons. Examples include using the phone to call the school, the teacher, or the doctor's office, shopping for food or cosmetic products, and applying for a job. Topics might be different from site to site and from year to year.

Once the topics are chosen, lesson plans are developed in collaboration with the parents. Lessons are specific to the site and to the English language proficiency of parents in the program. The emphasis is on oral communication in contexts in which program participants use English. When parents realize that they can use the English they are practicing in class, they begin inquiring about the proper way to say things, which provides authentic contexts and motivation for grammar lessons. Vocabulary that is chosen for study is authentic to everyday situations. Generic sentences are used to allow participants to practice their English in real life contexts.

Eventually, participants learn about different functions of writing and are given opportunities to practice different genres of writing. Parents often become interested in the role of written language and the value of keeping journals and doing creative writing. Each year a monograph of participants' writing is published. Writings can be in Spanish, English, or a combination of both since some parents do not feel comfortable writing in English. Other parents might use both languages as a stylistic decision. Also, depending on the topic, they might have a pref-erence for writing in one language or the other or both. When the parents are preparing their writings for the monograph, all FLAME writers participate in editing. At this time, they are introduced to gram-matical concepts in a contextualized and relevant manner.

Topics in the anthology vary by program site and school year. Some have written about their homes, keeping up a house, their children, their families in Mexico and Chicago, and their experiences coming to the United States. Samples of participants' writings from several FLAME monographs appear in Table 3.2.

Parents as Learners sessions are usually connected to Parents as Teachers sessions. For example, parents might write and make books for their children during the ESL class, an activity that increases home literacy opportunities and which is emphasized in several of the Parents as Teachers workshops.

Other FLAME Activities

The basic FLAME program as it was originally designed is described above. However, once the program was initiated, other modules were developed to complement the original program and to make it more rel-evant to the communities that it served.

Parents as Leaders

During literacy workshops, parents consistently raised issues that, although not related to literacy, were relevant to the families' daily lives. In order to meet this need and still keep the focus of the program on literacy, a beyond-literacy module was developed that is called Parents as Leaders. This module takes place as a summer leadership institute. During the year, each site keeps a record of relevant commun-ity issues that arise during ESL class discussions. Typically, toward the end of the school year, parents from all program sites decide on issues of interest to the family and/or the community that they would like to learn more about and understand better. Then, outside speakers are brought in to talk about those issues. Sessions are presented in the lan-guage that the parents know better. Some of the topics covered in recent summer institutes have included discipline at home, parents' rights, immigration, banks and their role in the community, and the use of hos-pital services. These topics also served to shape the content and proce-dures of other project activities.

Table 3.2 Sample of Parents' Writing

As participants in FLAME, parents become more confident of their English skills. They also discover new functions for writing in their daily lives. What follows are unedited samples of FLAME parents' writings. Pseudonyms are used rather than the real names of the writers. Spelling has not been edited.

Last month my dauther brok her elbow and we need to take her to te hospital. We was so scare because we don't now what was hapening whit her. When we get to the hospital to see the doctor she was criyin and we was so sed for her bat the doctor sed that was not so serius. He yes need to put a case on her.
Lucia C., 2001–2002

We would like you to know…
We are good mother's.
We are hard working people.
We want to study.
We are valuable.
We want to have better children.
We are constructive people.
Maria G., 2003–2004

I am from…
I am from Mexico.
I am an immigrant like most of yous.
I am going to try to learn to Speak English to my husband and I could keep our children without any trouble in school or with their homework.
Diana G., 2000–2002

Going to the Supermarket…
I need to go to the supermarket. I want to buy vegetables. The vegetables I need are corn, lettuce, tomato, potato, pepper, onion. Also, I need to buy meats. The kinds of meats I that I need to buy are pork chop, steak, chicken, fish, ham, ground meat. I need three pounds of each one. Also, I need fruit for my kids. The like eat bananas, apple, grape, orange. Also I need buy cereal, milk for their breakfast. Today, I want make rice with green beans. I need one can of this.
Iris C., 2002–2003

Hello, my name is Cindy B. and this is my little baby. Her name is Ariadna Castañeda. I have two daughters more. My baby has ten months old, and she have four teeth. She has a little hair. I'm 33 years old and my baby turns one year in two months. She is very, very funny.
Cindy B., 2002–2003

Winter Poem
I smell a hot chocolate cocoa.
I see the fall snow.
I hear the people sing.
I feel alegria and emotion in the Christmas.
I taste a sweet and hot ponche.
Zaida L., 2002–2003

Spring Has Sprung
Good bye cold wind
Good bye my jacket
Good bye the snow

Table 3.2 continued

Good bye to stay in the house
Good bye to the scarf
Ciao! The cold winter!
Marta A., 2002–2003

My Memories
I remember when I was young and I was living in Guanaguato Mexico with my family, my mother, my father, my three brothers and my little sister, every day my mother made homemade tortillas for us.

When I was young, I had many friends and in the afternoon we played games. I liked to ride my bicycle with my friends, I remember many things about my life in Mexico. but when I go to Mexico for vacations I miss the life in Chicago.
Sara A., 2005–2006

Dear teacher Carlos Ivan and friends from Project Flame:

I am Mario P, I am from Mexico, from San Luis Potosi. I like to do mechanical jobs and read books of Mexican history, especially legends. Currently, I work in a meat company, I am a meat packer. I have this job since 1996. I like to study English because is important to help my son with his homework. When I don't have to work, I spend time with my wife Maria, and I attend the English classes; she likes that, and I like it too. Thank you very much to the Project Flame!
Sincerely,
Mario P., 2005–2006

Vacation in Zacatecas Mexico
My favorite place to visit is Zacatecas because I was born there. It is an historic city. It is rich in minerals, it has big mountains, and a big church. When I go to Zacatecas, I like to taste the fresh food, like meats and fruits. When I go there, I walk for one hour everyday. When I go, I like to see my daughter play everyday. I never forget this time. Sometimes we visit different places. My daughter likes to visit my brother's house. After we return home, everybody feels happy.
Alma Z., 2005–2006

Immigration Debate 2006
I think this country is formed of a large part of immigrants. They find a better life and better future for their families, bet not everyone thinks this way. We are immigrants that find an opportunity to improve our life. The government labels us a weight to be carried, we are a problem for societies and for the improvement this country. But I think we are a big strength for the development of it. It is the men, after all, who make the laws. Why don't they think a little bit about the families that are being separated? We have our life formed here. We aren't terrorist, we aren't criminal, but sometimes someone we feel like it because don't have voice and vote. I agree that laws are very importants some case, because there are good as there bad. I hope that someday the government can accept us as part of this country. I hope that legislators work together for a united country and eliminate differences between people, to finish I think that this country is formed of immigrants and that is multicultural.
Lena M., 2005–2006

Training of Trainers

Another module that was developed in response to participants' concerns and needs is called Training of Trainers. It addresses the issue of capacity building in the community. This concept is important for nonprofit organizations in terms of maximizing the effectiveness of the program as well as developing competent leaders in the community. The goal of the module is to train people in the community who will be qualified to offer the program when the university is not available to provide services. Parents who have graduated from FLAME have the opportunity to develop further their literacy leadership activities in the community. Participants are parents who have completed two years in the basic FLAME program and show promise as literacy leaders. Training is provided for planning and implementing FLAME workshops that are relevant to parents in the community. To achieve this, trainees and university staff meet every other Friday to plan and develop materials and activities for the next session of FLAME to be offered at the program sites. During year one of the training, trainees serve as aides to university staff who implement the lessons. During year two, FLAME trainees are in charge of the workshops, with the assistance of the university staff. After two years, they receive a diploma stating that they have completed the training to become FLAME trainers. These parents are paid a fee for the preparation and implementation of the workshops during their training period. Several graduates have been successfully hired to provide family literacy training in schools in Chicago.

Parents as Volunteers

FLAME parents' desire to volunteer in their children's schools, and the teachers' uneasiness in allowing parents to serve as teachers in their classrooms led to the development of the Parents as Volunteers module. It has been instituted successfully at one school. Parents sign up in the principal's office to volunteer in classrooms. Then, the principal asks teachers if they need trained parent volunteers. Teachers who are interested give the FLAME program staff pertinent information, books, and any materials a parent might need, along with the days and times they would like a parent in their classroom. Parents are trained to present the lessons, and then they go to the classrooms and teach as planned.

Childcare

As part of program activities, FLAME graduates are hired to provide childcare for parents while they attend sessions and workshops. These graduates learn various educational activities that they can use with the children and also get paid for their services.

As can be noted, all FLAME activities allow participants to bring their own knowledge, ways of teaching/learning, and discourse into workshop discussions. Parents are encouraged to participate in the discussion in the language they know better. Program sessions are very interactive, and participants' ideas are valued and used during discussions in all components of FLAME but specifically, in the Parents as Teachers and Parents as Learners components of the program.

Summary

Several questions about parents and their role in their children's education were raised at the beginning of the chapter. These questions have been answered in the discussion. The following summary will serve as a reminder.

1. *How might parents support their children as they transition from home to school?*
   Family literacy programs are relevant to culturally and linguistically different families because they provide opportunities for connections between home and school and provide the children with a bridge that should facilitate their transition between home and school. This bridge allows for the practice of multiple cultural ways of learning; adds relevance to children's learning; and also allows parents to learn about the culture of the schools and about teacher expectations.

2. *Why is it important for today's schools to see parents as resources?*
   In a diverse society, it is imperative that teachers recognize the knowledge that children bring from home to school. It is also useful for teachers to use parents' knowledge to enhance the school curriculum. In these endeavors, parents and parents' knowledge can facilitate learning and support teachers.

3. *Why is it important for parents to partner with teachers in support of children's learning?*
   Through family literacy activities, parents learn about differences in cultural ways and discourse between home and school and they see the relevance of learning new practices to enrich the learning opportunities of their children. This will strengthen the bridge between home and school.

   Family literacy programs provide schools and teachers with opportunities to learn about parents' knowledge and to use that knowledge to support school activities that are relevant for the children. Also, as schools know more about parents in their community, they can plan activities for families and provide services in a timely and culturally relevant manner. This topic is discussed more in Chapter 6.

4. *Do schools need to rethink the ways in which they reach out to families? Why is this important today more than ever?*

    At a time of changing demographics, schools have to look at diversity issues other than race. The increasing multicultural and multilingual population in the schools means that schools must begin to address issues related to culture and language, particularly in regards to the curriculum and the home-community connection. We know that parents are willing to support their children's learning, but it is important that schools show the parents how to work together in this endeavor. Project FLAME, as described here, is an example of how schools could support parents' involvement in children's learning and in creating a bridge between home and school that will enhance children's educational opportunities and school success.

The parents' voices might be the best way to explain the success and impact of the program on participant families. The following are excerpts from parents' writing after two years of participation in the program. They have been translated from Spanish as faithfully as possible. Josefina relates how FLAME has helped her and her family:

> As any parent, I always thought learning should come to our children from teachers at school, the same as religion is taught by the priest at church. Participation in Project FLAME makes you aware how important it is to participate with the teachers in our children's education and be responsible for 50% of the learning because we are their first teachers. In my case, I have learned to communicate better with my husband and my daughter, but as a parent trainer, I have also learned to communicate with the community.

When asked whether children should learn to read at home, at school, or in both settings, Mercedes wrote:

> At both (home and school), because they will learn faster at school if we teach them a bit at home. What a child learns in school will not go over his head, if he already knows a bit. It is like climbing a ladder. If they know how or have an idea of how to climb, they will climb it quicker. If they have never climbed a ladder, they will not climb it fast.

Maria believes her children will do better at school because of what she learned in FLAME:

> They will do better because I teach them things that I learned in the program. For example, how to read. Before I used to teach them just the ABCs, and now I have learned different ways to teach them more effectively. For example, I use pictures from magazines and print in the community to teach literacy.

Chapter 4

A Sociocultural Framework in Support of Family Literacy Programs

Introduction

In Chapter 3, the components and activities that are part of Project FLAME were described so that the program could be used as context for a discussion of the home–school connection. In this chapter, I explain an important change that the program underwent after the initial few years. The original program design (content and activities) was developed according to what we (Rodríguez-Brown & Shanahan, 1989) believed parents needed to know and do in order to support their children's literacy learning at home. This is referred to as a "functional" program design (Rodríguez-Brown & Mulhern, 1993) because the program developers were outsiders to the community for which the program was intended. Also, the community did not have any input regarding areas of need and/or relevance to their concerns and interests as the program was developed.

The experience of working with Latino families in a community context made us aware of the need to listen to their voices and their concerns. This was necessary to keep the program relevant to the cultural group and to allow participants to use the information "critically" in their lives. The "critical" use of information refers to parents' understanding of the concepts presented to them, taking ownership of new knowledge acquired through the program, adapting it to their needs, and allowing that knowledge to support, not only the sharing of literacy with their children, but also their everyday lives. The need for participants to feel ownership of their new knowledge and their awareness of how this knowledge can enrich their lives is one of the reasons why we added modules to the original framework. This addition converted the FLAME program model from a functional to a critical model of family literacy. It seems that family literacy programs designed from a functional perspective tend to disappear unless they become critical to the participants' lives. In order to establish a critical perspective in programs involving adult learners (parents) and in dealing with adults who are culturally and linguistically different, it is necessary to acknowledge and connect with the knowledge that they bring to the learning situation. The program should support participants in finding ways to fit new learning into an already existing repertoire of cultural ways of learning.

While working with families through Project FLAME, it became apparent, at least to me, that these families brought a lot of knowledge to the program. I felt that we needed to recognize this knowledge and use it in the planning of program activities. I looked for support from current research that could justify and explain the need for programs that are directed toward linguistic minorities or other marginalized groups to acknowledge and respect the existing knowledge, ways of learning, discourses, and learning repertoires which these communities already possess. The work of Gee (1999), Gutiérrez and Rogoff (2003), Reese and Gallimore (2000), Rogers (2001, 2002), and The New London Group (1996), among others, led to and became the basis for the development of a sociocultural framework to further support program development for Project FLAME. The sociocultural framework should inform and underlie all program activities in order to make the program more relevant to the communities it serves. It also situates the program within a critical rather than functional perspective.

Cultural Ways of Learning

Discontinuities between cultural ways of learning at home and at school have been reported by a number of researchers (e.g., Moll, 1994; Purcell-Gates, 1995; Reese & Gallimore, 2000). Looking at specific cultures, Valdes (1996), Trueba, Jacobs, and Kirton (1990), Foster (1995), Laureau (1989), and Gallimore, Boggs, and Jordan (1974) have reported existing discontinuities in ways of learning between home and school for Latinos, Hmong, African Americans, working-class youth, and Native Americans, respectively. Also, Cazden (1986) and Tharp (1989) have documented existing discontinuities between home and school in such areas as linguistic codes, narrative patterns, motivation, participant structures, teaching strategies, and learning styles. These researchers identify and discuss variability between cultural groups.

Another researcher who has studied discontinuities is Heath (1983). She conducted a study of close communities in the Piedmont area of North Carolina and found that children in each of the three neighboring communities acquired a primary discourse that was specific to their community. In one community, children's home-based literacy was rich in analogies, group interactions, and storytelling, but it did not include activities such as book readings and school-like questioning experiences. In another community, children's home literacy included exposure to books of factual reality. Fantasy or fiction reading was discouraged as well as the comparison or transfer of ideas. The discontinuity between home-based literacy and school-based literacy made it difficult for children from these communities to succeed in school. However, in the third community, home literacy practices resembled school-based literacy practices. Heath found that children from this community were more successful in mastering school-based practices. Heath suggested that schools make accommodations for the types of literacy that children practice at home rather than focus only on middle-class family practices.

Not everyone shares this discontinuity perspective. Weisner, Gallimore, and Jordan (1988) criticized it and raised the issue of within group variability among people from the same ethnic group. Other critics (e.g., Chandler, Argyris, Barnes, Goodman, & Snow, 1985) have pointed out variability among people in different cultural groups in the ways they adapt to change and new circumstances. Issues of discontinuity are further clouded by a contrasting and deficit perspective, in which cultural ways of non-mainstream groups are seen as inadequate. Researchers such as Weisner (1997) and Gutiérrez and Rogoff (2003) believe that there is a problem with studying issues of discontinuity between home and school under the presumptions that culture is static and categorical, and that differences can be defined as traits.

These issues of discontinuity, individual variability, group traits, and cultural ways of learning have been studied from a variety of perspectives and with various approaches or models. Each perspective colors the analysis of the data and thus the results and interpretation of the researchers. Several of the perspectives are examined here.

Cultural-Historical Approach

Gutiérrez and Rogoff (2003) state that when culture is defined as static and categorical, it is difficult to study the relationship of individual learning to the practices of cultural communities. They call for an approach to the study of home–school discontinuities that takes into account the histories and valued practices of cultural groups—a cultural-historical approach to the study of learning at home versus learning at school. Within a cultural-historical approach, learning is studied as "a process occurring within activity" (p. 20), where there is not a separation between individual characteristics and the context where the activity takes place. Gutiérrez and Rogoff differentiate between identifying characteristics of individuals or groups and understanding the processes in the study of cultural ways of learning.

Cultural Models

In general terms, cultural models include the cultural and social resources that individuals or groups of individuals bring to their understanding of social situations (Rogers, 2001). Another definition describes cultural models as "storylines" or scripts that people have in mind when they engage in meaning-making activities (Gee, 1999). When literacy is involved in meaning making, the term can refer to resources that people have to interpret or produce texts (Fairclough, 1992). In regards to family literacy, cultural models influence not only what parents do with literacy in the home but how they do it.

Reese and Gallimore (2000) studied changes in beliefs and literacy practices at home with new immigrant Mexican families. They see culture as a flexible and dynamic construct rather than an unchanging and external force. In their study, they use a cultural model approach to studying learning at home, specifically early literacy development in children. This approach has been used before by other researchers, such as LeVine (1977), Weisner (1997), and D'Andrade (1995), in studying issues of socialization and child development.

Reese and Gallimore (2000) describe the effect that parents' views and beliefs about literacy have on the way they structure activities that support literacy learning at home. One belief is that children learn to read through repeated practice when they start school. Reese and Gallimore feel that this belief, or cultural model, is derived from the experiences of previous generations in rural ranchos where there was little formal schooling. This belief, along with others in the Latino cultural model, is brought by immigrants to the United States, and the model guides what they do with their children here.

Another finding of Reese and Gallimore was variability and flexibility within the cultural model. Previously, Gallimore and Reese (1999) reported that parents do not believe that their cultural model is static; rather, they see their beliefs as flexible and adaptable to new circumstances. From this perspective, the researchers view parents as "powerful agents of adaptation." According to Reese and Gallimore (2000), changes in the Mexican parents' cultural model for literacy development were not seen as threats to their traditional values. For example, once parents learned that reading to children at home supported literacy learning at school, they complied with teachers' assignments and suggestions.

Because of the flexible nature of the cultural model, Reese and Gallimore (2000) found that continuities and discontinuities co-exist in home–school literacy interactions. This finding contrasts with discontinuity explanations from previous research (e.g., Goldenberg & Gallimore, 1995), which describes discontinuities and no commonalities between learning at home and school as immigrant parents adapt to their new context. Reese and Gallimore (2000) conclude that:

> While parents did not initially share the teacher's view that reading aloud to young children was helpful in terms of their subsequent literacy development, they did follow through on teacher suggestions and requirements to read at home and appreciated the effects that this newly appropriated activity had produced.
>
> (pp. 130–131)

In this situation continuity between home and school was created in response to teachers' requests and not just from parents' observations in the new environment. Perhaps the viewpoint that cultural models are flexible helps to explain why new immigrant parents were willing to modify and adapt their cultural ways in a new context in response to teachers' requests.

This case is an example of what can be accomplished through family literacy training, particularly in situations where parents' cultural ways are accepted and new practices are taught and discussed with them as they become more involved with their children's education and learn more about school expectations for parents in U.S. schools. From my perspective and experience with culturally and linguistically diverse families, this kind of acceptance and training are required for the process of adaptation to be effective.

Discourse

Discourse can be seen as a theoretical construct that provides a way to examine discourse practices and explain mismatches and discontinuities that often separate home and community discourse from that of the schools and other social institutions (Gee, 1996). Differences in discourse are described by Gee (1999), who makes a distinction between d (discourse) which refers to linguistic aspects of language defined as "language-in-use or stretches of language (like conversations or stories)" (p. 17), and D (Discourse) which includes linguistic aspects of language and also beliefs, sociocultural issues, and political issues related to language. Gee calls D "language plus 'other stuff'" (p. 17). The "other stuff" includes beliefs, symbols, objects, tools, and places connected to a particular identity. Gee believes that discourses do not have discrete borders. They can split into one or more discourses, or several discourses can meld together. New Discourses can appear and old Discourses can disappear.

According to Gee (1996), children acquire their primary discourse at home and in the community by exposure, immersion, and practice. As children learn their primary discourse, they also learn ways of believing, practicing, and performing literacy. Children must learn a secondary discourse when they come in contact with social institutions such as schools.

The discourse construct has been used to explain the mismatch or the discontinuity that exists between home and school for culturally and linguistically different children (Moll, Amanti, Neff, & Gonzalez, 1992; Purcell-Gates, 1995). Purcell-Gates (1995) and Teale (1986), among others, believe that children whose primary discourse is similar to the school discourse are able to adjust to school easier and faster and can be more successful than children whose primary discourse is very different from the discourse of school. Usually mainstream children's primary discourse closely resembles school discourse.

However, children from culturally and linguistically diverse families bring to the school setting primary discourses that are different from the mainstream. Learning the secondary discourse of school is more tenuous for those children. In other words, children who have the least trouble in the transition between home and school come from homes and communities where the discourse and cultural ways of learning are similar to those used in school settings.

Another researcher who employed the discourse construct is Rogers (2003), who describes a case study of literacy practices in an African American family. Building on the work of others (i.e., Delpit, 1995; Erickson, 1993; Gee, 1996; Heath, 1983; Mercado & Moll, 1997), Rogers (2003) situates her research on family literacy practices "within the cultural discursive mismatch social debate" (p. 4). She describes the discourse mismatch as a "lack of alignment between the culture, language and knowledge of working-class students and dominant institutions such as schools" (p. 5). Rogers uses the discourse construct because she felt that none of the typical responses reported by other researchers explain the mismatch.

Rogers (2003) recognizes that differences might occur as part of literacy learning in the home when there is an intergenerational transfer of ideologies about schooling and parents' work rather than through a difference between primary and secondary discourses. In her case study she found that a conflict existed between discourse communities for her subjects due more to "fragmented subjectivities" (p. 154) in the family literacy practices of the mother as she worked with her children at home. Although the values, beliefs, and actions of the schools were represented in the home practices, reading and writing were seen as individual endeavors that were judged, measured, and valued by someone other than the individual. Rogers believes that more equitable schooling would make space for the literacy that is learned and used at home and in the classroom.

Multiliteracies

The New London Group (1996) has been developing a theoretical framework to deal with classrooms where teachers have to negotiate a multiplicity of primary and secondary discourses, as well as the multiple subjectivities (interests, intentions, and purposes) that students bring to the learning situation. The theoretical framework tries to connect the "what" and "how" of literacy pedagogy within the changing social environments of classrooms. From the New London Group perspective, when students face a learning situation, they have to design new meanings and remake themselves within historical and cultural patterns of meaning.

It is important, then, that teachers accept what students bring to the classroom and provide them with multiple pedagogical perspectives to learn. The New London Group discusses the limitations of using only situated practice as a classroom methodology. They explain the need to include overt instruction, in which students gain knowledge, and critical framing, which requires students to think and make connections with what they learned. These two steps lead to transformed practice, which can enhance learning in multiliteracy settings.

Implications of a Sociocultural Framework

There are several points that teachers, school personnel, and program directors and developers should keep in mind when planning or working with diverse parents and communities:

- Culturally and linguistically different parents have a lot of personal knowledge that they share with their children.
- They might use cultural models of sharing that are different from mainstream practices.
- They might use a language other than English.
- They bring different primary discourses and literacies into communities and into programs such as FLAME.

Family literacy programs should recognize these differences and use them as starting points for what is taught or shared through the program. Sociocultural research-based programs, such as FLAME, need to add to the repertoires that parents bring to the program, including new linguistic and cultural practices and knowledge, rather than try to change parents' existing practices.

Summary

Family literacy programs which function within the sociocultural framework described here should:

1. Accept and validate the parents' native language and the knowledge they bring into the program.

2. Welcome and embrace differences in cultural learning models, discourse, and literacies.
3. Make program participants aware that knowledge acquired through the program is to be added to their existing knowledge and repertoire.
4. Recognize that not all knowledge is acquired only in English, and parents should share literacy with their children in the language they know better.

Using this theoretical framework, we have developed program practices for Project FLAME that add new activities to family literacy practices while respecting and supporting ways that parents teach their children at home. The following set of principles guides all program activities:

- Let families know that their contributions to their children's learning are important and wanted.
- Allow parents to use the language they know better in all project activities and encourage them to use that language at home to support their children's learning.

    A Teaching Assistant (TA) reported that this principle was a very important aspect of the FLAME program because of the language stigma that exists in Chicago. Parents that she worked with often brought up concerns regarding home language use. Many parents worried that if they used Spanish at home, their children would not learn English as well. Given that the parents identified this as a concern, the TA brought in some research on second language acquisition and led a discussion about how strength in the native language aids in second language learning. In this way, the FLAME program allowed parents to learn more about a topic that was relevant to them, as well as become more confident in their own abilities to support their children's learning.

- Accept all knowledge that participants bring to the learning situation.
- Use families' cultural ways of learning/teaching as steppingstones to new learning.

    One example of this principle is evident in the Songs, Games, and Language Literacy Session. The session begins by asking parents to share some of the songs that they teach their children. Then parents discuss why this is important and what children learn when they sing songs. Many parents realize that songs help children learn new words and about the concept of rhyming. At this point, the facilitators can ask parents to reflect on how these skills relate to literacy learning. Through the conversation that ensues, parents learn that when children learn rhymes, they are also acquiring the ability to recognize and distinguish between different sounds in the language. Although parents might not understand the words phonemic awareness, this discussion allows them to talk about it using their own discourses while increasing their own understanding of why these activities are important in literacy development.

- Connect with the knowledge that participants bring to a learning situation in order to make new knowledge more relevant for participants.
- Add, rather than subtract, new knowledge and interaction to already existing repertoires in families and the community.

   Many parents report that they share books with their children. When asked what they do after finishing a book, parents discuss having the child retell it or asking the child their opinion of the book. Here, facilitators could validate and encourage parents to continue these practices. The discussion might then be led into other strategies that parents could use to help increase their children's comprehension of stories.

- Use funds of knowledge and cultural ways already existent in the community to structure program activities in order to enhance the program effectiveness.

   One group of TAs reported the inclusion of a time for parents to share community resources that are relevant in each literacy session. This "forum" is a time for parents to share their experiences and knowledge regarding available resources. For example, in the Book Sharing Literacy Session one parent talked about and brought in materials about a summer program at the local library in which her son had participated. Other parents were very motivated to hear about the program and asked many questions about it. This was also an empowering experience for the parent who shared her experiences in that program and became a resource for other FLAME parents. Thus, in this way the FLAME program allows parents to see themselves as part of a community that helps and supports one another.

- Expose program participants to multiple pedagogies as they learn how to provide their children with knowledge that supports their children's transition from learning at home to learning at school.

In Project FLAME we follow these principles in all our activities and believe they are one of the reasons for our success for 19 years. In the next chapter, data collected from the program is used to demonstrate the program's effectiveness.

Chapter 5

Effectiveness of the FLAME Program

Introduction

In order to fulfill evaluation requirements for the Office of Education, the original funding agency for Program FLAME, an evaluation design was developed in 1989 to study the effectiveness of the program. Since then, data have been collected and analyzed yearly. The results have been used in reports to funding agencies and foundations and in a number of publications (Rodríguez-Brown, 2001a, 2001b, 2003, 2004; Rodríguez-Brown, Li, & Albom, 1999; Rodríguez-Brown & Meehan, 1998). The database used for the analysis and description presented in this chapter includes information about parents and their target children who participated in Project FLAME from fall of 1999 to spring of 2005. Also included are data from a comparative study of FLAME and non-FLAME participants' children, which was conducted in 1992. At that time, the results met a requirement of the state of Illinois to qualify for Academic Excellence status. This status led to the program becoming a national model and to a dissemination grant.

Results of a more recent comparison are also presented. During the last two years (2004–2006), the state of Illinois has required that all public schools test their pre-school and kindergarten children in order to qualify for Reading First grants. Most of the children of FLAME parents are of pre-school or kindergarten age, so test results are used to compare the performance of FLAME participants' children with all tested children at their respective schools.

In addition, through the years, observational data have been collected from a small group of families to learn about the uses of literacy at home and whether parents exhibit changes in literacy behaviors as a result of their participation in FLAME. Descriptive data were analyzed and some of the findings are reported in this chapter.

All data have been collected following the proper human subjects procedures required by the University of Illinois and approved by the Chicago Public Schools. Parents provided written consent for all the procedures followed according to the research protocol approved for the research and evaluation done with Project FLAME subjects.

Instruments and Data Collection

Each year, as families are recruited to participate in the program, parents are interviewed to check their eligibility for the program, which includes having a child between three and nine years old. If a family has more than one eligible child, the parents choose one child, preferably of pre-school age, who is designated the target child. Prospective participants also complete a questionnaire, which asks for demographic data, literacy activities of the family, and the availability of literacy-related materials at home. Another section requires parents to rate statements that correspond to the four components of FLAME, using a Lickert scale (from 1 to 3, with 3 being the highest rating). The purpose of the ratings is to learn about parents' interest in, and knowledge about, different components of the family literacy program prior to starting the sessions. The same questionnaire is administrated again at the end of each school year. Participant parents are also pre-tested and post-tested each year on their English proficiency skills using the Adult-LAS (Language Assessment Scale) (De Avila & Duncan, 1993). The results of the LAS are used initially for placement in appropriate levels of ESL instruction. The post-tests provide information about how participants' language proficiency changes during a year in the program.

As a result of their participation in FLAME workshops, parents are expected to provide more educational opportunities for their children at home, which in turn should help their children be more successful in school. Target children from participant families, ages three to nine, are administered the following assessments to evaluate growth in school readiness and achievement as a result of their parents' participation in the literacy program:

- Letter Recognition Test. This test consists of uppercase and lower-case letters. The raw scores indicate the number of letters recognized by the child. The test is administered in Spanish to children who are three to six years old.
- The Boehm Test of Basic Concepts (Boehm, 1986). This test measures concept development (time, quantity, etc.) as evidence of cognitive development. The test is administered in both Spanish and English (different versions) to avoid confounding lack of English or Spanish proficiency with concept development. Children in kindergarten or first grade are given the school-aged version of the test, while younger children, three to five years old, take the pre-school version.

- Print Awareness Test (The Stones/Piedras Test developed by Marie Clay, 1979). This test is given in Spanish to children who are three to six years old and measures their knowledge of print conventions, such as directionality (reading from left to right).
- LAS-English Language Proficiency Test and the Pre-LAS (De Avila & Duncan, 1987; Duncan & De Avila, 1986). These tests measure the child's oral and aural proficiency in English. The Pre-LAS is given to children four to six years old. Children in first grade are administered the LAS-Oral Language Proficiency Test.

These instruments are suited for the population participating in the program. The tests are administered in Spanish, except for the LAS tests which measure English proficiency.

Children are tested at the beginning of the school year before their parents have received any FLAME literacy training and again at the end of the school year after their parents have completed the program. The pre-test and post-test design is used to examine what effects parents' participation in FLAME might have on their children's emergent literacy skills.

Characteristics of FLAME Participants from 1999–2005

Although the demographic data for parents involved in FLAME vary from year to year, the variation is minimal. Therefore, demographic information for the school years 1999–2005 is combined for the present description. A total of 767 parents and/or grandparents were served by the program during those years. Most of the parents (97%) were born in Mexico, and 87.6% of the families reported that they used primarily Spanish at home. On average, mothers in these families had been in the United States for 8.74 years, while fathers had been here for an average of 12.33 years. The average age for mothers was 33.01, and fathers, 36.02 years. Finally, mothers reported that they had finished an average of 8.56 years of schooling, while fathers reported 8.51 years of schooling.

For self-reported language proficiency levels, both mothers and fathers felt their reading proficiency in Spanish was good/very good (84.1% and 85%, respectively) and their writing proficiency was good/very good (74.1% and 83.7%, respectively). In English, 94.6% of mothers reported their reading proficiency as none or very little, and, for writing, 72.4% reported none or very little proficiency. For fathers, 69.2% reported none or very little writing skill in English, and 63.9% reported none or little reading skill in English. These findings served as justification for providing family literacy workshops in the language the parents know better: Spanish.

Data Analysis and Results

In order to show the effectiveness of Project FLAME as a family literacy program, information related to target children from participant families is presented first. Even though children are not direct participants in the program, we believe that what parents learn in the program benefits their children indirectly. Second, results are discussed from parents' self-reports of literacy uses at home before they started the program and at the end of one year, as well as their improvement in English language proficiency.

FLAME Effectiveness in Children

The database for 1999–2005 includes data from 734 target children three to nine years old who were tested over the six-year period. (Note: Due to a change in the design of data collection, post-tests were not administered for 2002–2003.) Table 5.1 shows the mean pre-test and post-test scores for all children who took the pre-test, the post-test, or both.

Of the children in Table 5.1, only 430 of them took both pre-tests and post-tests. Table 5.2 shows a T-test comparison between pre-test

Table 5.1 Mean Scores of Target Children on Pre-Tests and Post-Tests in These Measures

Measures	N	Mean	S.D.	Minimum	Maximum
Pre-Test					
Letter Recognition–Uppercase	702	9.59	9.63	0	28
Letter Recognition–Lowercase	701	9.53	10.12	0	32
Print Awareness (Piedras)	600	6.96	7.55	0	24
Pre-school Boehm–English	341	5.11	6.26	0	26
Pre-school Boehm–Spanish	306	10.84	4.12	1	19
School-age Boehm–English	379	13.20	8.41	0	25
School-age Boehm–Spanish	381	17.98	6.44	0	25
Pre–LAS	506	12.99	16.88	0	51
LAS	161	7.73	2.84	0	14
Post-Test					
Letter Recognition–Uppercase	441	11.61	8.65	0	28
Letter Recognition–Lowercase	440	12.34	10.07	0	32
Print Awareness (Piedras)	523	9.88	6.76	0	24
Pre-school Boehm–English	312	6.63	5.80	0	24
Pre-school Boehm–Spanish	306	14.60	3.66	6	22
School-age Boehm–English	240	21.12	4.42	0	25
School-age Boehm–Spanish	240	22.83	4.14	0	25
Pre–LAS	370	13.67	13.23	0	59
LAS	155	11.32	2.20	7	15

Table 5.2 A T-Test Comparison of Pre-Test and Post-Test Scores of Children in These Measures

Measures		Mean	N	S.D.	T-Value
Letter Recognition–Uppercase	Post	11.52	430	8.55	23.782*
	Pre	6.60	430	8.31	
Letter Recognition–Lowercase	Post	12.27	429	10.00	20.874*
	Pre	6.34	429	8.59	
Print Awareness (Piedras)	Post	8.61	409	6.73	18.915*
	Pre	5.16	409	6.03	
Pre-school Boehm–English	Post	6.49	308	5.60	8.956*
	Pre	3.44	308	2.93	
Pre-school Boehm–Spanish	Post	14.60	306	3.66	13.506*
	Pre	10.84	306	4.12	
School-age Boehm–English	Post	21.26	227	4.20	16.509*
	Pre	12.91	227	8.73	
School-age Boehm–Spanish	Post	23.15	228	3.59	12.708*
	Pre	18.43	228	6.03	
Pre-LAS	Post	12.46	345	12.42	21.485*
	Pre	7.06	345	13.39	
LAS	Post	11.32	155	2.20	14.295*
	Pre	7.74	155	2.78	

Notes
*significance at .001 level.

and post-test scores in the nine literacy skill areas that are tested for children who took both tests. The significant T-values for all literacy areas were at the .001 level, which means that we can claim with 99% confidence that these children performed better in the post-testing. After a year of their parents' participation in Project FLAME, children could recognize significantly more Spanish uppercase and lowercase letters and had more awareness of print conventions. They also knew more Spanish and English words and could speak English more fluently. Based on the results, we feel with some confidence that children whose parents participated in FLAME have benefited from their parents' newly acquired knowledge.

Because there might be other factors that influence performance, pre-test and post-test comparisons are not the best way to show program effectiveness. However, these results seem to show that parents in Project FLAME are making a difference in preparing their children for schooling in the United States. It is important to explain that the majority of the children tested were not participating in any school or community-based intervention or other program that might affect the test results.

A Comparative Study of FLAME and Non-FLAME Children

One of the problems with collecting data from children in projects like FLAME is that it is usually very hard to find a comparison group of children whose parents do not attend a family literacy program. During the 1991–1992 school year, one of the public schools that was a Project FLAME site allowed us to test a group of children who were attending their pre-school program, which was funded by the state of Illinois. This program was offered to a limited number of children who were considered low SES and at-risk of failing in school. The parents of these children did not participate in FLAME or other interventions at the school.

The same tests that are used with FLAME children were administered to the pre-school children, thus providing a comparison group. This arrangement allowed a quasi-experimental design to compare the children of FLAME parents (N=18), who were not in a formal school program, to a comparison group of children (N=21) attending a state-funded pre-school program. The two groups of children were equivalent in age (four years old), ethnicity (Mexican), home language (Spanish), and neighborhood (same for both groups). Children in the comparison group, however, came from families with a higher SES, with parents reporting more stable employment and income. They also were more successful in finding community resources, such as the pre-school program, for their children. Parents of both groups signed informed consent for their children to be tested. The children were administered the Letter Recognition Test, the Boehm Test, and the Clay Print Awareness Test (Piedras) in October of 1991 and again in May of 1992. All tests were administered in Spanish, since the children were mostly Spanish speakers.

Results of data analysis comparing the two groups appear in Table 5.3. A look at pre-test scores for both groups shows that FLAME children scored significantly lower on the lowercase letter recognition test, at the .001 significance level, and on the test of print awareness at the .02 significance level. Differences in the test of uppercase letter recognition were substantial and at the .07 significance level. Again, the control group scored higher. The difference between the groups on the Boehm Test was minimal.

In order to control for preexisting differences between the FLAME and the comparison group, an analysis of covariance (ANCOVA) was conducted, using the pre-test scores as a covariate to adjust the post-test results. The variance of homogeneity of the two groups was equal when tested as part of the analysis of covariance procedure. The results indicate that no significant differences in performance existed at post-test, as shown in Table 5.3.

Table 5.3 Comparison of Differences Between FLAME Children and a Control Group on Four Measures

Measure	Flame[a]			Control[a]				
	Pre	Post	Pre	Post	F	(df)[b]	p
Uppercase Letters	2.62 (5.9)	11.50 (9.9)	5.34 (6.4)	11.79 (9.7)	.592	(1.39)	.444
Lowercase Letters	1.49 (5)	9.75 (9.2)	4.31 (4.9)	9.17 (8.4)	.698	(1.39)	.409
Print Awareness	2.49 (4.3)	7.56 (5.4)	7.81 (2.5)	10.7 (4.2)	1.07	(1.39)	.307
Boehm	42.86 (6.6)	47.00 (4.0)	42.43 (6.4)	47.00 (4.5)	.854	(1.39)	.792

Notes
a F-tests were based on comparisons of group performance after pre-test differences were statistically controlled.
b n = 18 for FLAME group, n = 24 for control group.

The use of a control group in this study provided information about whether the increases in children's performance were the result of parents' participation in FLAME and not simply that of normal development, maturation, learning, or exposure that all children experience. Although FLAME children lagged behind the comparison group in several areas related to early literacy learning at pre-test, they generally "caught up" during the months their families participated in FLAME. They managed to do this despite the fact that comparison group children were attending a formal pre-school program and FLAME program children were not enrolled in an educational program.

In spite of the pre-test/post-test comparisons, the results of this small study provide some information about the effectiveness of Project FLAME. In 1993, data from this study were presented in a report to the Illinois State Board of Education's Office of Community Programs, Early Childhood Education and Bilingual/ESL Education, in order for FLAME to be nominated as an Academic Excellence Program (Rodríguez-Brown & Mulhern, 1993).

The results also support the notion that creating a home environment that is rich in literacy, as parents do in FLAME, can increase children's achievement. Clearly, children can acquire literacy skills while their families are involved in the program, even though the children do not experience any direct FLAME program intervention, and even though their immigrant parents typically have limited literacy skills themselves, limited experience with school, and limited English proficiency. Parents in Project FLAME are definitely making a difference in preparing their children for schooling in the United States.

A Comparison with the ISEL

More recently, under provisions of the No Child Left Behind Act of 2001 (United States), public schools have been required to administer early literacy tests to children in their pre-school programs. This requirement enables a comparison of the performance of children from FLAME participants to the performance of all four-year-olds in a specific school.

During the 2003–2004 academic year, one of the schools participating in Project FLAME gave the Spanish version of the Illinois Snapshot of Early Literacy (ISEL) (Illinois State Board of Education, 2004) to their Spanish-speaking pre-school students who were four years old, including children of FLAME participants. The Spanish ISEL measures eight early literacy skill areas, which are alphabet recognition, story listening, phonemic awareness, one-to-one matching and word naming, letter sounds, developmental spelling, word recognition, and graded reading passage. Table 5.4 contains the pre-test and post-test mean scores of both FLAME and non-FLAME children.

The results indicate that FLAME children had higher mean scores than non-FLAME children in most of the literacy skill areas at both pre-test and post-test. This is especially evident in alphabet recognition and story listening, where FLAME children had much higher mean scores than non-FLAME children. These results might suggest that FLAME parents have had more interactions with their children in such literacy events as teaching ABCs, sharing books with children, and talking about books—activities which parents have learned through FLAME workshops.

To determine whether FLAME children scored higher than non-FLAME children as a result of their parents' participation in the literacy project, an ANCOVA was employed (see Table 5.5). Adjusted post-test mean scores of FLAME children were still higher than those of non-FLAME children. Differences were found in alphabet recognition, phonemic awareness, and one-to-one matching and word naming, although the results were not statistically significant. An ANCOVA of letter sounds, developmental spelling, word recognition, and graded reading passage could not be done because the number of FLAME children who took both pre-tests and post-tests in these areas was four, less than the five required for any statistical analysis.

A dependent T-test was also performed to determine whether the FLAME children at that school had made progress in Spanish literacy skills during the school year. The results, shown in Table 5.6, reveal that these children had higher post-test mean scores than pre-test mean scores in all of the literacy skill areas. The differences in alphabet recognition, phonemic awareness, and one-to-one matching and word

Table 5.4 Mean Scores of Pre-Test and Post-Test on Spanish ISEL by Non-FLAME and FLAME Pre-School Students

Measures	Non-FLAME Children			FLAME Children		
	Mean	N	S.D.	Mean	N	S.D.
Pre-Test						
Alphabet Recognition	15.13	95	18.15	26.43	7	21.79
Story Listening	9.66	95	4.52	11.71	7	3.04
Phonemic Awareness	5.41	135	2.44	6.20	10	2.49
1-to-1 Matching and Word Naming	4.96	135	2.94	4.50	10	2.84
Letter Sounds	16.18	65	7.19	16.40	5	8.26
Developmental Spelling	16.29	65	10.83	19.20	5	13.48
Word Recognition	7.54	65	8.06	6.20	5	8.67
Graded Reading Passage	1.75	65	3.10	2.40	5	5.37
Post-Test						
Alphabet Recognition	47.43	101	8.55	53.00	7	1.15
Story Listening	12.87	101	4.35	14.29	7	4.99
Phonemic Awareness	8.44	101	1.88	9.29	7	0.76
1-to-1 Matching and Word Naming	8.23	101	2.66	8.57	7	0.79
Letter Sounds	22.36	140	4.44	21.80	10	6.05
Developmental Spelling	27.83	139	10.68	28.10	10	14.20
Word Recognition	19.04	75	5.80	17.60	5	8.74
Graded Reading Passage	8.32	76	4.66	7.40	5	4.51

Table 5.5 Adjusted Post-Test Mean Scores on Spanish ISEL of Non-FLAME and FLAME Children using ANCOVA

Measures	Group	N	Pre Mean Score	Post Mean Score	Adjusted Post Mean Score	F-Value
Alphabet Recognition	Non-FLAME Children	86	16.53	47.45	47.59	1.376
	FLAME Children	7	26.43	53.00	51.32	
Story Listening	Non-FLAME Children	86	9.38	12.88	12.99	0
	FLAME Children	7	11.71	14.29	12.97	
Phonemic Awareness	Non-FLAME Children	86	4.83	8.41	8.42	0.998
	FLAME Children	7	5.57	9.29	9.12	
1-to-1 Matching and Word Naming	Non-FLAME Children	86	4.09	8.33	8.33	0.041
	FLAME Children	7	4.29	8.57	8.54	

Table 5.6 T-Test Comparison of Pre-Test and Post-Test Scores of FLAME Children on Spanish ISEL

Measures		Mean	N	S.D.	T-Value
Alphabet Recognition	Post	53.00	7	1.15	3.141*
	Pre	26.43	7	21.79	
Story Listening	Post	14.29	7	4.99	1.430
	Pre	11.71	7	3.04	
Phonemic Awareness	Post	9.29	7	0.76	3.495*
	Pre	5.57	7	2.64	
1-to-1 Matching and Word Naming	Post	8.57	7	0.79	3.873**
	Pre	4.29	7	2.98	
Letter Sounds	Post	19.50	4	9.04	1.035
	Pre	15.00	4	8.83	
Developmental Spelling	Post	26.25	4	17.58	1.015
	Pre	18.00	4	15.25	
Word Recognition	Post	16.75	4	9.84	2.005
	Pre	6.25	4	10.01	
Graded Reading Passage	Post	7.50	4	5.20	1.732
	Pre	3.00	4	6.00	

Notes

* significance at .05 level, ** significance at .01 level.

naming were significant at both the .05 and .01 level. However, caution must be used when interpreting the mean scores for letter sound, developmental spelling, word recognition, and graded reading passage because results from a small sample size are not reliable.

A Comparison Using the DIBELS Test

During the 2004–2005 academic year, all four-year-olds who attended Early Reading First programs in Chicago Public Schools were required to take the Dynamic Indicators of Basic Early Literacy Skills (DIBELS) tests in English. The DIBELS (Good & Kaminsky, 2002) is administered to students in K through sixth grade three times a year: at the beginning, middle, and end of the academic year. Since the DIBELS measures similar literacy skill areas as Project FLAME, DIBELS scores for FLAME children can be used to help validate the findings of their literacy skills as measured through the project assessment tools. DIBELS scores can also be used to compare the literacy skills of FLAME children with their non-FLAME peers in the same schools. The comparison will help determine whether FLAME children perform better due to their parents' participation in the project.

A total of 26 FLAME children from the four schools with a FLAME program took the DIBELS tests during the 2004–2005 school year, with six children in kindergarten, eight in first grade, and 12 in second grade (see Table 5.7).

The DIBELS mean scores of the FLAME children by grade level are presented in Table 5.8. For comparison purposes, the mean scores of their non-FLAME peers are also presented. Although kindergarten and first-grade FLAME children scored lower on some subtests at the beginning of the year, they scored higher than the non-FLAME students in all but one subtest at the end of the year. It is interesting to note that

Table 5.7 DIBELS Assessment Schedule by Grade at FLAME Participating Schools

Measures	Beginning of Year (b) Month 1–3	Middle of Year (m) Month 4–6	End of Year (e) Month 7–10
Initial Sounds Fluency (ISF)	K	K	
Letter Naming Fluency (LNF)	K, 1st grade	K	K
Phonemic Segmentation Fluency (PSF)	1st grade	K, 1st grade	K, 1st grade
Nonsense Word Fluency (NWF)	1st grade, 2nd grade	K, 1st grade	K, 1st grade
Oral Reading Fluency (ORF)	2nd grade	1st grade, 2nd grade	1st grade, 2nd grade

Table 5.8 Mean Scores of DIBELS Measures of FLAME and Non-FLAME Children by Grade

Measures	FLAME Children			Non-FLAME Children		
	Beginning	Middle	End	Beginning	Middle	End
Kindergarten (six FLAME children and 78 non-FLAME children)						
Initial Sounds Fluency (ISF)	2.67	6.40		5.06	6.63	
Letter Naming Fluency (LNF)	3.33	11.00	16.83	4.34	4.80	18.87
Phonemic Segmentation Fluency (PSF)		2.40	19.50		1.63	14.12
Nonsense Word Fluency (NWF)		9.40	22.17		5.57	15.14
First-grade (eight FLAME children and 111 non-FLAME children)						
Letter Naming Fluency (LNF)	11.63			13.15		
Phonemic Segmentation Fluency (PSF)	14.63	17.88	28.25	8.84	14.09	21.87
Nonsense Word Fluency (NWF)	11.50	26.88	55.63	9.68	28.04	44.63
Oral Reading Fluency (ORF)		11.50	29.88		11.94	27.19
Second-grade (12 FLAME children and 113 non-FLAME children)						
Nonsense Word Fluency (NWF)	66.92			51.87		
Oral Reading Fluency (ORF)	46.50	65.33	65.92	27.11	42.65	56.03

second-grade FLAME children outperformed their non-FLAME peers in NWF and ORF at every testing period.

In order to investigate whether FLAME children did better than non-FLAME children as a result of their parents' participation in the literacy project, another ANCOVA was employed. This statistical procedure examines the differences between groups in the post-test mean scores after controlling for the differences in the pre-test mean scores. If a difference is significant in the adjusted post-test mean scores, it might be due to intervention. Obviously the analysis requires both pre-test and post-test data. As shown in Table 5.7, some of the DIBELS tests were given only once; some twice, and others three times during the school year. In order to meet the pre-test and post-test requirement of the ANCOVA, the first test was used as the pre-test and the last test as the post-test if a test was given three times during the year. If a test was given twice, the scores from the first test were considered as pre-test and the second as post-test scores. If a test was given only once, the scores from the test could not be included in the analysis because the data does not meet the pre-test and post-test requirement. Table 5.9 reports the results of the ANCOVA.

Although none of the differences in mean scores were statistically significant, as indicated by non-significant F-values in Table 5.7, the ANCOVA results show that, overall, FLAME children were able to achieve higher scores than non-FLAME children at the post-testing. FLAME children were also able to catch up with their peers when they initially had lower scores in some literacy areas. Obviously, FLAME children have made progress in early literacy skill acquisition.

To determine whether the progress was significant, a dependent T-test was applied. The pre-test mean scores of FLAME children were compared with their post-test mean scores on the same measures. The results, shown in Table 5.10, reveal that FLAME children had higher post-test mean scores in all of the literacy skill areas. Although not all of the differences were significant, there is evidence that kindergarten FLAME children made significant improvement in letter and phonemic awareness, and first-grade FLAME children had significant growth in learning letter/sound relationships and oral reading proficiency.

Results from the standardized DIBELS tests administered by the schools validate the findings from FLAME literacy assessments. FLAME children had significant and/or faster development in literacy skills. This might be related to the intervention of the FLAME family literacy program because parents had learned how to teach these skills to their children throughout project activities.

Table 5.9 A Comparison of Adjusted Post Mean DIBELS Scores Between Non-FLAME and FLAME Children Using ANCOVA

Measures	Group	NN	Pre Mean Score	Post Mean Score	Adjusted Post Mean Score	F-value
ISF (kindergarten)	Non-FLAME Children	53	3.43	6.75	6.67	0.034
	FLAME Children	5	1.40	6.40	7.26	
LNF (kindergarten)	Non-FLAME Children	76	4.39	18.82	18.67	0.000
	FLAME Children	6	3.33	16.83	18.67	
PSF (kindergarten)	Non-FLAME Children	54	1.63	7.59	7.68	2.097
	FLAME Children	5	2.40	15.00	14.09	
NWF (kindergarten)	Non-FLAME Children	54	5.57	8.48	8.71	2.561
	FLAME Children	5	9.40	21.00	18.51	
PSF (1st grade)	Non-FLAME Children	109	8.75	21.87	22.03	0.609
	FLAME Children	8	14.63	28.25	26.07	
NWF (1st grade)	Non-FLAME Children	109	9.76	44.63	44.76	0.646
	FLAME Children	8	11.50	55.63	53.89	
ORF (1st grade)	Non-FLAME Children	108	11.99	27.30	27.26	0.316
	FLAME Children	8	11.50	29.88	30.37	
ORF (2nd grade)	Non-FLAME Children	113	27.11	56.03	57.93	2.036
	FLAME Children	12	46.50	65.92	48.03	

FLAME Parents' Home Literacy Practices and Attitudes

Participants in Project FLAME completed a questionnaire regarding their home literacy practices and attitudes toward literacy at the beginning and end of each school year. Although there are shortcomings to self-reporting, it was the only way to collect the type of data needed. Table 5.11 shows a frequency distribution of the parents' pre-program and post-program responses to questions regarding home literacy practices. Since the number of parents completing the questionnaire was not

Table 5.10 A T-Test Comparison of Pre-Test and Post-Test Scores of FLAME Children on the DIBELS

Measures		Mean	NN	S.D.	T-Value
ISF (kindergarten)	Post	6.40	5	5.18	1.814
	Pre	1.40	5	3.13	
LNF (kindergarten)	Post	16.83	6	13.09	2.712*
	Pre	3.33	6	8.17	
PSF (kindergarten)	Post	15.00	5	9.67	3.896*
	Pre	2.40	5	4.34	
NWF (kindergarten)	Post	21.00	5	21.94	1.243
	Pre	9.40	5	11.30	
PSF (1st grade)	Post	28.25	8	12.06	2.128
	Pre	14.63	8	16.47	
NWF (1st grade)	Post	55.63	8	28.59	5.871***
	Pre	11.50	8	14.18	
ORF (1st grade)	Post	29.88	8	20.30	4.457**
	Pre	11.50	8	10.68	
ORF (2nd grade)	Post	65.92	12	39.60	1.955
	Pre	46.50	12	34.08	

Notes

* significance at .05 level, ** significance at .01 level, *** significance at .001 level.

the same at the beginning and end of the school year, percentages are also reported.

Parents' responses were analyzed using a T-test to measure whether the improvements were significant. Table 5.12 shows that the means of the year-end questionnaire responses were almost all significantly higher at the .001 or .01 level. At the end of the program, parents showed their children signs and words in the street or market more often and used library cards to check out books for their children since more parents obtained a library card. Also, they read more books, newspapers, and magazines, and their children saw them reading and writing more often. Parents and children read books to each other and talked about books together more often. They also encouraged their children to write with more frequency. Parents knew much more about how to teach the ABCs and how to choose a book for their children. Obviously, the data show that the program has achieved one of its main objectives—to support Latino parents in learning how to provide literacy opportunities at home and help their children succeed in school.

FLAME Parents and the Home–School Connection

Since one of the components of the FLAME program includes activities that are designed to enhance the relationship between home and school,

Table 5.11 Frequency Distribution of Parents' Responses to Pre-Program and Post-Program Questionnaires

Questions	Answers	Responses to Pre-survey		Responses to Post-survey	
		N	Percent	N	Percent
Literacy Opportunities					
How often in the week do	1 = almost never	53	7.7	17	3.5
you show your child signs	2 = sometimes	425	61.8	190	39.6
or words in the street or	3 = all the time	210	30.5	273	56.9
market?					
Do you have a library card?	1 = no	279	40.1	20	4.1
	2 = yes	417	59.9	462	95.8
How often do you use your	1 = almost never	235	37.7	19	4.5
library card every month?	2 = sometimes	288	46.2	221	52.7
	3 = all the time	100	16.1	179	42.7
How often do you check	1 = almost never	225	34.4	123	25.8
out books from the library	2 = sometimes	327	50.0	240	50.4
for your child every month?	3 = all the time	102	15.6	113	23.7
Literacy Modeling					
How often do you read	1 = almost never	100	14.4	10	2.1
books, newspapers,	2 = sometimes	430	61.8	215	44.4
magazines?	3 = all the time	166	23.9	259	53.5
How often does your child	1 = almost never	32	4.6	5	1.0
see you reading to yourself?	2 = sometimes	391	56.6	146	30.2
	3 = all the time	268	38.8	333	68.8
How often does your child	1 = almost never	19	2.8	8	1.7
see you writing?	2 = sometimes	448	65.1	217	44.9
	3 = all the time	221	32.1	258	53.4
How often do you write	1 = almost never	83	12.0	22	4.5
letters, messages, or lists	2 = sometimes	390	56.2	304	62.8
every month?	3 = all the time	221	31.8	158	32.6
Literacy Interaction					
How often do you read	1 = almost never	30	4.4	4	0.8
books to your child?	2 = sometimes	430	62.6	299	62.0
	3 = all the time	227	33.0	179	37.1
How often does your child	1 = almost never	91	13.6	69	14.6
read to you?	2 = sometimes	350	52.4	245	52.0
	3 = all the time	227	34.0	157	33.3
How often do you and your	1 = almost never	27	3.9	9	1.9
child talk about books?	2 = sometimes	428	62.4	276	57.4
	3 = all the time	231	33.7	196	40.7
How often do you	1 = almost never	5	0.7	1	0.2
encourage your child to	2 = sometimes	230	33.5	71	14.6
write?	3 = all the time	452	65.8	413	85.2
Literacy Competence					
How much do you know	1 = almost nothing	51	7.4	10	2.1
about teaching the ABCs	2 = some	375	54.4	154	32.4
to your child?	3 = a lot	263	38.2	311	65.5
How much do you know	1 = almost nothing	52	7.5	17	3.6
about choosing a book for	2 = some	503	72.8	234	49.0
your child?	3 = a lot	136	19.7	227	47.5

Table 5.12 T-Test Comparison of Parents' Pre-Program and Post-Program Responses on Literacy Usage

Questions		Mean	N	S.D.	T-Value
Literacy Opportunities					
How often in the week do you	Post	2.55	423	0.56	9.401**
show your child signs or words	Pre	2.23	423	0.58	
in the street or market?					
Do you have a library card?	Post	2.04	431	0.31	14.860**
	Pre	1.62	431	0.53	
How often do you use your	Post	2.42	345	0.57	12.375**
library card every month?	Pre	1.81	345	0.68	
How often do you check out	Post	1.95	416	0.71	5.466**
books from the library for your	Pre	1.78	416	0.69	
child every month?					
Literacy Modeling					
How often do you read books,	Post	2.55	431	0.53	13.044**
newspapers, magazines?	Pre	2.03	431	0.61	
How often does your child see	Post	2.71	429	0.47	10.647**
you reading to yourself?	Pre	2.39	429	0.56	
How often does your child see	Post	2.54	426	0.53	8.607**
you writing?	Pre	2.31	426	0.48	
How often do you write letters,	Post	2.32	433	0.50	0.267
messages, or lists every month?	Pre	2.31	433	0.62	
Literacy Interaction					
How often do you read books	Post	2.36	425	0.49	4.865**
to your child?	Pre	2.24	425	0.52	
How often does your child read	Post	2.18	417	0.68	3.020*
to you?	Pre	2.09	417	0.67	
How often do you and your child	Post	2.39	426	0.52	5.079**
talk about books?	Pre	2.25	426	0.52	
How often do you encourage	Post	2.87	427	0.34	10.051**
your child to write?	Pre	2.59	427	0.51	
Literacy Competence					
How much do you know about	Post	2.66	420	0.52	9.174**
teaching the ABCs to your child?	Pre	2.34	420	0.62	
How much do you know about	Post	2.46	426	0.56	10.509**
choosing a book for your child?	Pre	2.12	426	0.48	

Notes

* significance at .01 level; ** significance at .001 level.

the questionnaire that parents complete at the beginning and end of the school year includes questions about the role of parents in supporting their children's readiness for school. It also covers questions about home–school relationships. Table 5.13 presents the frequency distributions for parents' pre-program and post-program responses to these questions.

Table 5.13 Frequency Distribution of Parents' Pre-Program and Post-Program Responses about Surveys

Questions	Home-school Connection				
	Answers	Responses to Pre-survey		Responses to Post-survey	
		N	Percent	N	Percent
How much do you know about what your child learns in preschool and elementary school?	1 = almost nothing	59	8.8	24	5.1
	2 = some	313	46.8	160	33.9
	3 = a lot	297	44.4	288	61.0
How do you feel when talking to your child's teachers?	1 = uncomfortable	95	14.1	13	2.7
	2 = comfortable	374	55.3	134	27.9
	3 = very comfortable	207	30.6	333	69.4
In your opinion how much can you help your child at school by reading books together at home?	1 = almost nothing	22	3.2	9	1.9
	2 = some help	243	35.7	179	37.6
	3 = a lot	416	61.1	288	60.5
How often does your child bring home homework every week?	1 = almost never	20	3.0	4	0.9
	2 = sometimes	95	14.1	46	9.8
	3 = all the time	557	82.9	420	89.4
How often do you help your child with his/her homework every week?	1 = almost never	20	3.0	9	1.9
	2 = sometimes	189	27.9	167	35.0
	3 = all the time	468	69.1	301	63.1
How often do you participate in your child's school activities every year?	1 = never	107	16.0	27	5.7
	2 = 1–2 times	255	38.1	166	35.2
	3 = more than 3 times	307	45.9	278	59.0
How often did you talk to your child's teacher?	1 = never	81	12.4	17	3.6
	2 = 1–2 times	149	22.8	102	21.8
	3 = more than 3 times	424	64.8	349	74.6

At the end of one year in FLAME, a higher percentage of parents reported learning much more about their child's learning in schools. They also reported feeling more comfortable talking to their child's teachers. A higher percentage of parents felt that they could better support their children's learning by reading books together at home and helping their children with homework more often than before they attended the FLAME program. They also reported more parental participation in school activities and talking more often to their child's teachers.

Significant T-values (see Table 5.14) show differences in parents' attitudes regarding their role as teacher in their children's literacy learning, their knowledge about what their children learn in school, their willingness to talk to their children's teachers, and their ability to support their children's literacy learning at home.

Table 5.14 T-Test Comparison of Parents' Pre-Program and Post-Program Responses about Home–School Connections

Questions		Mean	N	S.D.	T-Value
How much do you know about what your child learns in preschool and elementary school?	Post	2.56	409	0.59	6.893**
	Pre	2.33	409	0.66	
How do you feel when talking to your child's teachers?	Post	2.70	420	0.52	15.165**
	Pre	2.12	420	0.66	
In your opinion how much can you help your child at school by reading books together at home?	Post	2.59	424	0.53	2.081*
	Pre	2.53	424	0.57	
How often does your child bring home homework every week?	Post	2.90	416	0.32	5.229**
	Pre	2.75	416	0.49	
How often do you help your child with his/her homework every week?	Post	2.62	427	0.51	1.177
	Pre	2.59	427	0.55	
How often do you participate in your child's school activities every year?	Post	2.56	417	0.59	7.377**
	Pre	2.25	417	0.78	
How often did you talk to your child's teacher?	Post	2.72	408	0.51	
	Pre	2.40	408	0.78	8.125**

Note

* Significance at .05 level; ** significance at p .001 level.

The self-reported responses of parents showed that their participation in Project FLAME activities enhanced their understanding of the home–school relationship and the uses of literacy at home. In addition, parents seemed to better understand the need to interact with teachers and the school in order to support their children's learning.

Parents' Improvement in English Literacy

As part of the Parents as Learners component, FLAME parents participate in ESL classes to learn English or to improve their English proficiency and skills as they become literacy learning models for their children. Each year, new parents in FLAME are administered the Adult-LAS Test (De Avila & Duncan, 1993) before they start in the program and at the end of the school year. The Oral Language section of the LAS assesses listening comprehension and oral language proficiency in English. The Reading Proficiency section measures reading ability in terms of fluency, mechanics, reading for information, and vocabulary.

Table 5.15 shows the mean scores of parents who took the LAS as a

Table 5.15 Pre-Program and Post-Program Mean Scores of FLAME Parents on the A-LAS

Measures	N	Mean	S.D.	Minimum	Maximum
Pre-Program					
Oral–Vocabulary	556	9.40	8.85	0	40
Oral–Conversation	555	3.37	2.98	0	10
Oral–Sentence Completion	555	3.62	3.84	0	14
Oral–Total	551	16.34	12.58	0	59
Reading–Vocabulary	573	4.71	2.50	0	10
Reading–Fluency	573	4.81	2.47	0	10
Reading–Reading for Information	573	4.83	3.12	0	10
Reading–Mechanics	573	7.66	4.71	0	20
Reading–Total	572	22.02	10.60	0	49
Post-Program					
Oral–Vocabulary	439	12.34	8.59	0	40
Oral–Conversation	439	4.20	2.99	0	10
Oral–Sentence Completion	439	5.74	4.25	0	14
Oral–Total	437	22.10	11.72	1	56
Reading–Vocabulary	489	5.65	2.72	0	10
Reading–Fluency	489	5.31	2.93	0	10
Reading–Reading for Information	489	6.55	2.60	0	10
Reading–Mechanics	489	9.43	5.03	0	20
Reading–Total	489	26.97	11.59	1	50

pre-test and post-test. For all subtests, the mean scores at the end of the year were higher than at the beginning of the year. In other words, parents performed better in both oral and written English on the post-tests than they did on the pre-tests.

A T-test was used to compare pre-test and post-test mean scores. Table 5.16 shows significantly higher post-test mean scores in almost all of the English oral and reading areas examined by the LAS. After one year of participation in the Parents as Learners component of FLAME, which emphasized ESL within a participatory approach, FLAME participants knew more vocabulary, completed more sentences, read more fluently, understood more information through reading, and had a better knowledge of English mechanics, even though the ESL lessons did not emphasize formal instruction in grammar and academic English.

T-test results indicate significant gains in each subtest related to oral language and reading, but not for conversation. This result is unexpected since anecdotal evidence suggests that parents learn a great deal through the participatory approach. Because the approach is functional to their lives, they also enjoy the lessons while they are learning. The unexpected scores might be the result of a mismatch between the way the test measures conversation and the way conversation is taught in the program.

Table 5.16 A T-Test Comparison of Pre-Program and Post-Program Test Scores of FLAME Parents on the A-LAS

Measures		Mean	N	S.D.	T-Value
Oral–Vocabulary	Post	11.34	391	8.10	4.502**
	Pre	9.67	391	8.84	
Oral–Conversation	Post	4.24	391	2.93	–0.603
	Pre	4.32	391	2.69	
Oral–Sentence Completion	Post	6.20	391	4.24	7.109**
	Pre	4.86	391	3.83	
Oral–Total	Post	21.56	389	11.58	4.741**
	Pre	18.88	389	12.32	
Reading–Vocabulary	Post	5.41	418	2.71	6.763**
	Pre	4.45	418	2.47	
Reading–Fluency	Post	5.04	418	2.96	2.133*
	Pre	4.70	418	2.39	
Reading–Reading for Information	Post	6.39	418	2.69	12.007**
	Pre	4.48	418	3.05	
Reading–Mechanics	Post	9.06	418	4.95	6.025**
	Pre	7.45	418	4.52	
Reading–Total	Post	25.94	417	11.69	8.508**
	Pre	21.12	417	10.14	

Notes

* Significance at .05 level and ** significant at .001 level.

Summary of Analysis and Results

The analysis of quantitative data collected between 1999 and 2005 from both FLAME participants and their children showed that participating in family literacy activities through FLAME resulted in a number of differences in practices and attitudes, as well as achievement for both parents and children. By the end of each year in the FLAME program, participants knew more about how to teach literacy at home and in the community, and they found many opportunities to share literacy with their children. They knew how to use play and games for learning things such as the ABCs. They were more familiar with library resources, and they knew how to choose books to share with their children. They learned more about interacting with their children while reading books or sharing knowledge. They also seemed to understand principles of emergent literacy better, and they began to accept their young children's attempts to read and write. They participated more in school activities, interacted more with their children's teachers, and felt more comfortable doing so. They knew more about what their children learn in school, and they felt more confident supporting their children's learning at home. Most importantly for the children, and themselves, was the fact that they knew that they could teach their children more effectively using their cultural ways of learning and also the language they knew better.

Observational Studies

Over a number of years, qualitative information, mostly from observations and field notes, had been collected on a small sample of FLAME families. These data were used to validate and complement findings from the analysis of self-reported information from parents and the testing data discussed earlier. In addition, several other observational studies have been conducted.

Case Studies

In 1991, a FLAME staff member who had worked with parents for several years decided to study the literacy behaviors of three Project FLAME families and to document any changes in family literacy behaviors during the year they attended the program (Mulhern). The families for the study were chosen because they had a good attendance and participation record in program activities.

All three families in the study were considered low-income. Each family had a child enrolled in pre-school. One of the mothers had much more education than the other two and had been a kindergarten teacher's aide in Mexico. Mulhern visited the families six times during the year to observe literacy activities in their daily lives. Field notes were taken during those observations, and artifacts of children's writings were collected. Literacy interactions with the children, interviews, and book sharing sessions were tape-recorded and transcribed. During one of the last visits, parents were asked to read a book of their choice with their children, and they were interviewed further about their literacy practices. Observations of the three parents were also conducted at FLAME sessions. Patterns that emerged from Mulhern's (1991) data corresponded mainly with three of the four theoretical components of Project FLAME.

Literacy Modeling

The three families exhibited a great range of literacy modeling. The Fernandez family, who had the highest level of education among the three families, used literacy for various purposes, including reading for pleasure. The Diaz and Morela families used literacy primarily to fulfill daily living routines (e.g., paying bills) and school-related functions (e.g., doing homework, reading school notices).

Literacy Opportunities

The FLAME program emphasizes the importance of making writing materials and books easily available to children. Mulhern's home visits revealed that the accessibility of these materials at home was critical for their use. Even though Mrs. Morela did not have many books, she kept the literacy box (developed through FLAME) and books on a table in the living room. This placement resulted in the frequent use of these materials by the children. The Fernandez' home had the broadest range of literacy materials available, which were also conveniently located. In both of these homes, children read and wrote frequently during Mulhern's visits.

However, in the Diaz' home, the few books that were available were kept in a closet in the bedroom. The target child never used them during the observations.

Literacy Interactions

FLAME workshops teach parents techniques that enable them to engage more effectively in literacy activities with their children. Mulhern's examination of two major aspects of literacy in the home, shared book readings and emergent writing, revealed varied patterns of parent-child interaction among the families she studied.

Mulhern observed that all of the children were read to at home. Furthermore, it was clear that the children were familiar with the books they had at home, and they were accustomed to having books read to them. This finding is significant due to the widespread understanding that read alouds increase children's learning about literacy (Teale, 1984; Wells, 1986). In general, parents read materials that were appropriate for their children's ability and interest levels. They read with expression and seemed to enjoy the books as much as their children did. In addition, parents used a variety of strategies to get their children involved in the reading. They asked questions, checked for understanding, asked labeling questions, and related the books to the children's lives. Thus, the children were active participants in the book readings. Two of the target children also engaged in reading-like behaviors, which are considered learning-to-read strategies (Doake, 1985). Also, all children engaged in pretend reading which helps children to reconstruct written text (Pappas & Brown, 1988).

One of the major revelations from Mulhern's (1991) observations at FLAME sessions was that the parents bought books in English rather than Spanish at the FLAME book fair. This occurred in spite of the fact that all of the parents had been encouraged to read to their children in the language they knew better. This practice allows parents to serve as good reading models for their children. Instead, the parents that Mulhern observed translated the text into Spanish as they read the books to their children. This meant that they could not point to words in the book since they were not reading the actual English words. Consequently, the children were deprived of opportunities to connect oral language to written language as they listened to a favorite book. A further problem was that the parents were not proficient in English and sometimes had to check the dictionary or ask someone else for the equivalent word in Spanish. Since then, FLAME workers have frequently emphasized the need for parents to read books to their children in the language they know better. Not only can parents read more fluently in their native language, but also children have the opportunity to match oral and written language as books are read to them (Teale, 1986).

Mulhern also looked for evidence of parents and children writing in the homes. When discussing emergent writing, FLAME personnel encourage parents to include children in their writing activities and to recognize children's written approximations as meaningful. However, this was a difficult concept for the parents to understand, since they retained traditional beliefs about writing. To them, writing meant penmanship, not composition. They believed that children needed to learn to write the letters correctly first before they could actually write texts. This was more evident in Mrs. Diaz's family, although it also appeared to a lesser extent in the other families. Mrs. Diaz explained that her son wrote letters, not words. She felt that her child would learn to read easier if he knew how to write the letters well.

Parents in the other two families eventually accepted their children's emergent writing as meaningful. Mrs. Morela specifically explained that she had learned this from FLAME. Her daughter engaged in writing more frequently than the other two children in the observed families. The mother usually recognized her daughter's intention to write as meaningful and praised her literacy approximations. Although all parents received the same training from FLAME, they exhibited a range of understanding about emergent writing. This range is difficult to explain.

Recent Observations

During the 2001–2002 academic year, FLAME staff resumed the study of literacy use in families who participate in FLAME, using the same methodology as in the previous study. Families were visited three times a year, and field notes of the observations were analyzed to learn about how the families used literacy at home.

One of the families being studied, the Castillo family, provided insight into the literacy life of FLAME families who have both school-aged and pre-school children. Again, this family was chosen for the observational study because of their attendance record and participation in Project FLAME activities. In the Castillo family, the school-aged children, who knew English quite well, assumed the role of reading in English to the younger child. The mother tended to use community resources to enhance the literacy skills of the pre-school child. Although the family did not have many books at home, except for school textbooks and some books acquired through FLAME, they decided to purchase a computer. The children played games on the computer, but the father, who had been a dentist in Mexico, used it to teach science to his school-aged children while he practiced English with them.

In this family, literacy learning was important for everyone, but there were well-defined supporting roles for different members of the family. Mrs. Castillo was so involved in family literacy that she asked to be accepted in the Training of Trainers module. She is currently becoming a family literacy leader in the community. In addition, the influence of the father's job-related knowledge on literacy learning in this family seems to confirm and support previous research findings by Reese, Gallimore, and Goldenberg (1999) regarding the extent to which parents can be involved in literacy activities with their children in the home.

Summary of Observational Studies

Data that Mulhern (1991) collected from the case studies showed that FLAME had an impact on the availability and use of reading materials in the homes. Parents were aware of the importance of reading to children, and children enjoyed reading together with their parents. Also, among the families studied, two out of three realized the value of getting their children interested in books as a way to support their learning to read. In general, FLAME staff reported that once parents understood that children can learn from books before they are able to read independently, parents' attitudes about allowing the children to handle books changed. Parents also learned to use the library and borrow books to increase the availability of books at home.

Recent case study data has revealed the different roles that family members might assume during literacy practices in the home. In some families, the mother is the main source for modeling and interaction, but other family members can also play a significant role in literacy development and in learning English.

Networking, Self-Efficacy, and Project FLAME Participants

In my work with the immigrant Latino community in Chicago, I have learned that new families often have very isolated lives, even in communities that share their language and culture. New immigrants are usually separated from family and friends by their move to the United States. As a result, mothers seldom leave the house except to drop off their children at school. They spend their days cleaning house and watching television. They only go out with their husbands, mostly on Saturdays and usually to do laundry and go shopping for food.

The isolation of new immigrants was not foreseen in the planning stage of FLAME, but as the program was implemented, we discovered how important it is that families have the opportunity to network. Developing new social networks takes time and energy, and the FLAME sessions provide a safe setting for that to happen. However, networking activities go beyond family literacy workshops and ESL classes. These families develop friendships that are sustaining, supportive, and lasting.

In FLAME sessions, we validate the parents' native language and knowledge as a way to get them excited about sharing literacy with their children at home. During program activities, we encourage parents to share their cultural models of learning, discourses, and literacies with other parents, and at the same time, we provide them with new information that they can add to their existing repertoire. In order to facilitate the parents' use of their own cultural ways of learning, we involve a group of former FLAME participants in the planning of program activities. We also allow participants to discuss what would be the best ways to interact with their children while sharing literacy with them. By building on parents' awareness of their own cultural and family knowledge, we enhance their sense of self-efficacy. This increased belief in their own ability to produce change affects not only their role as teachers for their children, but also their lives in the community and in society.

Before becoming involved in FLAME, many of the mothers in our program never left their house without their husband. Since their work in FLAME, they have been able to make friends, go to the library, and take public transportation. FLAME is a family literacy program, but it has impacted families in unplanned ways that go beyond literacy. During the last two years, several personal experiences have illustrated for me the beneficial effects of self-efficacy and networking on these families.

Two years ago, while attending a conference in Arizona, I met two community organizers who work with a powerful school reform group in Chicago. After I introduced myself, I was surprised when they asked me if I was the Director of Project FLAME. Then, they told me that they had hired two graduates of the FLAME Training of Trainers module. They added that, so far, these mothers have proven to be the best leaders they have hired for working with the schools and the community.

Last year, at the beginning of the school year, I visited several Chicago public schools to invite parents to participate in Project FLAME. One of the schools had invited other participant organizations to the meeting, and, to my surprise, three of the speakers making presentations to parents for community organizations were recent graduates of Project FLAME. One of them, full of pride, told me that his son had been accepted at MIT and had left Chicago the week before to attend classes there.

Finally, during this summer, a worker who has been involved in FLAME since 1989 reported her experience while attending a concert at the Ravinia Summer Festival, a well-known summer concert series in Highland Park, Illinois. She was surprised to find that six women from one of our FLAME sites were employed at the concert park. As she talked to one of these parents, the mother explained that since two of them now drive cars, they share rides when they commute to work. She also stated how thankful she was for what she had learned through FLAME.

I am fairly certain that it was not the English they learned in FLAME classes that supported these women in their lives. I believe that the networking they started while participating in FLAME activities facilitated their way out of the community and their search for jobs. The self-efficacy these women gained while supporting their children's literacy learning at home expanded to include obtaining jobs and a sense of fulfillment they never imagined.

Chapter 6

Program Development, Implementation, and Practice in Family Literacy

Introduction

The data presented and discussed in the previous chapter examined various kinds of learning that occurred with parents, especially literacy behaviors at home which indirectly benefit children's early literacy learning and cognitive development, even though children are not the main focus of the program. Also, the participant parents improved significantly in their English proficiency, not only in oral language but in reading and writing.

This chapter discusses a different kind of learning that has occurred as a by-product of the program, learning by program staff about how to develop and implement programs for culturally and linguistically differ-ent families and communities, especially Latino communities. Personally speaking, working with parents and children from Project FLAME has been a very enriching learning experience, something which cannot be learned from simply reading books about the subject. The focus of this chapter is the knowledge that I have acquired through 19 years of work with mostly new immigrants in the Latino community in Chicago. It has been through my interactions with parents from Project FLAME during all those years that I have learned a great deal about ways in which family literacy programs can address more effectively the needs of linguistically and culturally different families. I also discuss some of the issues that are critical to the success of programs directed toward English language learning populations, with an emphasis on new Latino immigrant groups.

Discussions with Latino Parents

Parents' Role as Teachers

During the early years of Project FLAME implementation, I had the opportunity to discuss with groups of parents their role as teachers. To my surprise, I discovered that they did not see themselves in that role. Parents explained that they were not or could not be teachers because they did not have much schooling and they did not know English. When I asked them whether there were things they could teach their children at home, they talked about cooking, sewing, going to the store, reading labels, writing letters, and making lists. Suddenly, they realized that not all knowledge comes from schooling. They also realized that they did not need to use English in order to support their young children's literacy learning at home. Immediately, I sensed a change in attitude and increased self-efficacy. Parents realized that they were already teachers for their children. This experience led me to decide that an important requirement in working with culturally and linguistically different parents is the need to validate their language and knowledge so as to strengthen their belief in their role as the first and most important teachers of their young children.

Once their children started attending school, however, a dichotomy developed about parents' role in teaching and supporting their children's learning. At that point, parents differentiated between their roles in educating versus teaching their children. For them, the Spanish words "educar" (to educate) and "ensenar" (to teach) have very distinct and specific meanings. Parents saw their role as one of "educar" (to educate) their children, which means to help them become good people by teaching them morals, manners, and values. The school's role, on the other hand, was that of "ensenar" (to teach) math, reading, science, and other subjects. I later learned that this dichotomy, and the parents' ambivalence toward their role as teachers in support of their school-aged children's learning had been encountered by other researchers (Reese et al., 1995; Valdes, 1996).

Another issue that parents faced when they felt themselves pressured to fulfill the role as teachers was related to the concept of "respeto." This concept is discussed widely by Valdes (1996). Teachers are highly regarded in the Latino culture, and parents feel that they should not interfere with or intrude upon the role of the teacher. Furthermore, they were not sure that teachers wanted immigrant parents to help their children at home. Recent findings from a longitudinal study by Reese and Gallimore (2000) show that teachers' explicit demands for Latino parents to read to their children at home as part of daily homework had a positive affect on the families' behaviors and on their view of literacy development. They found that although parents showed specific cultural ways of learning and teaching to support their children at home, they were able to learn and use new strategies and activities, so long as they were not in conflict with family values and morals.

Language and Learning: Parents' Concerns

Dealing with parents' concerns about language differences between home and school was not as easy as explaining their potential role as teachers. Parents for the most part thought that if they lived in the United States, they should teach their children in English. This belief led to a discussion of what is important for supporting children's development of early literacy and how this process is more cognitive than language specific. However, I did not talk about cognition with the parents. Rather, I explained that they needed to help develop the child's brain (a concept they understood), and that whatever they taught their children in Spanish would help the children once they learned English at school. We also talked about the need to provide good language models in English, in order for children to learn English well. From these conversations, parents learned that they could and should share their knowledge with their children, and they could do it in their native language which they knew better.

Learning about Context and Families

An understanding of these concepts could not have been gained from reading books and journal articles. FLAME parents have been great teachers in my endeavors to support them as the most important teachers for their young children. They have made me realize the importance of knowing and including the context for a family literacy program in the design and development of that program. I have learned that designing programs requires more than what I, as a literacy researcher and teacher, think these parents need to learn. Many programs that stay at this level, which I call "functional" (Rodríguez-Brown & Mulhern, 1993) disappear quickly unless parents begin to take an active role in the planning of program activities. Family literacy programs need to change and adapt to the needs of the populations served. In essence, flexibility should be a characteristic of the program. This is not to say that the assumptions underlying the program design or the content has to change. The focus of the original program design might stay in place. Rather, it is the implementation and delivery that changes.

I do not believe that there is a specific family literacy program that will fit all populations. Some national programs that mandate specific components for everyone show high rates of attrition and low attendance, despite the fact that adequate funding is available. The reason for this level of performance might not be parents' lack of interest in a literacy program, but rather that some aspects of the programs are incongruent with the culture of some families. For example, programs that require home visits might not be popular with Latinos. This is due to the fact that fathers usually work during the day, and they do not want anyone visiting their home unless they are present. Mothers who want to learn how to support their children's learning might have to withdraw from programs that have home visits as a required activity. Home visits can be successful in Latino communities when the program staff have a long-term relationship with the family and are respected in the community.

Insights Gained about Latino Families

Isolation

While working with the Latino community, I learned about how socially isolated new immigrant families are, even when they live in neighborhoods where their native language is spoken. This is something we did not realize when we planned the activities for FLAME. As the program was implemented, however, we discovered the value that networking has for these families. In terms of implementation, this means that program activities have to be very interactive to allow families to learn from each other. Also, participants need opportunities to share their experiences and knowledge. A program that focuses only on what the developers think parents have to learn might not be successful in Latino communities.

Parents' Voices and Concerns

Parents want their voices to be heard and their cultural ways of acquiring and sharing literacy acknowledged and valued. As discussed earlier, programs that validate the parents' language and knowledge enhance their sense of self-efficacy and their involvement in their children's learning. Programs that rely on written instructions or "short-term" training are not very effective with this population (Reese & Gallimore, 2000). Program activities should allow parents to demonstrate their current practices and talk about what they do at home and in the community in support of their child's early literacy learning. Allowing parents to bring homemade books to class or show alternative, cultural ways of interacting with their children is one way of validating parents' knowledge and accepting their cultural models of learning.

Concept of "Familia"

The concept of "familia" (Abi-Nader, 1991) is central to everyday life in Latino communities and is especially important to new immigrant families. This concept means that whatever is done in everyday life should benefit not only the individual, but also the family. For example, if mothers do something for themselves, such as attending classes to learn English, they think of ways that their increased fluency in English will help the family, particularly the children. This is one of the reasons why I believe that family literacy programs are a better alternative to adult education programs in Latino communities (Rodríguez-Brown & Meehan, 1998).

Since most fathers work during the day and have fairly rigid work hours, they are not usually able to attend ESL classes or FLAME sessions. Although many mothers also work, they more often have flexible work hours so they tend to participate more regularly in family literacy program activities. This does not mean that fathers are not involved. Fathers attend and participate actively in FLAME functions such as field trips and book fairs. They also attend special celebrations and, of course, graduations.

Because of the importance of family, scheduling activities should be conducted with input from potential participants. In Project FLAME, the participants, mostly mothers, have decided that they prefer to meet in the morning when they bring their children to school. That is when they feel more secure walking in the community. They feel safe in the schools, and their husbands see the school as a safe setting for their wives.

As part of program development, we have discussed the possibility of meeting in the evenings or on Saturdays in order to include fathers or other adults at home, but this has not been feasible because of conflicts with the daily schedules of the families we serve. Other programs do meet in the evenings (Paratore, 2001), and they are well attended. The important point is that decision-making at all levels should include the voice of potential program participants at each site and should take into account the interests of all members of the family.

Family considerations also have implications for enrollment and activity planning. To be of the most benefit to Latino populations, family literacy programs should include activities for all members of the family. This enhances attendance and retention of parents as participants in a program, since they are likely to attend more regularly if they feel that the program is for the whole family.

Depending on the time of day when program activities take place, it might be necessary to plan activities for other members of the family in addition to the parents who are participants in the program. In the case of Project FLAME, we know that mothers will not attend unless they can bring their pre-school-aged children with them. Since only a few activities in the program are intergenerational (e.g., shared readings), we offer childcare for young children who attend the program with their mothers.

Childcare

There are two important issues regarding childcare with Latino parents. First, parents have to trust the caregiver. A person who is well-known in the community or a mother with grown children is more acceptable than a stranger. We usually consult with parents before we choose the caregiver, and usually hire from among people who have graduated from FLAME and know how to support children's learning. For some parents, it takes a while before they get to know and trust the childcare personnel enough to allow their children to attend childcare. One surprising fact is how well-behaved these young children are when they stay with their mothers in class. They show a lot of "respeto" for the fact that their mothers are in school and learning.

A second issue is the need for organized childcare. Mothers want their children involved in creative learning activities while in childcare. In FLAME, we provide training in such activities for childcare givers. We also provide supplies so that children of different ages can be involved in non-structured, age-appropriate learning activities, while their mothers attend FLAME sessions. During the summer, when we offer beyond-literacy leadership activities for parents, all of the children in the family come to the program, so we also have to plan activities for school-aged children. All childcare givers are compensated for their services.

Defining Family

When we started the implementation of Project FLAME in 1989, the Amnesty Program (a program that allowed undocumented individuals to receive visas to work) required that applicants attend ESL classes to improve their English skills. In Latino communities, most ESL classes were full, and enrollment was closed to new students. When we provided ESL classes as part of FLAME, we had more people than we expected attending our classes. At that point, we had to start asking ourselves questions about how the people attending our ESL classes were related to the FLAME families. The high enrollment also raised the issue of extended family in the Latino culture, which could include first, second, and third cousins, and their cousins and friends. For the program to be effective, and in order to meet the needs of FLAME families, we defined family as parents, children, and grandparents enrolled in the program. It was also important to clarify that FLAME was a program intended for parents of children three to nine years old, and that it was a family literacy program rather than an adult education or ESL program. Through the years, we have kept this definition of family when identifying participants for Project FLAME. We also make it clear to prospective FLAME parents that the program teaches family literacy as well as ESL, and participants must take an active role in both components.

Insights about Program Implementation

Over the years I have learned much about program implementation and gained insights that might apply to family literacy programs with other cultures, not just Latino communities. The next section addresses some of these concepts and issues. Sometimes the understanding is about what not to do as well as what works.

Recruitment and Retention

Although FLAME is a community program based in the public schools, program sessions and activities do not always take place in a school. Through the years, we have moved some programs to park district facilities due to a lack of space in public schools. Also, in the park district settings we have been able to serve several schools at one site. However, no matter where the program activities take place, we have learned that the public school connection is very important for recruitment purposes.

Another thing we have learned is that neither mailings nor the telephone are good methods of recruitment. Many times families do not receive mail because they do not have a mailbox, or their names are not listed as tenants. We also have found that many families cannot afford a telephone. Furthermore, new immigrant families might move often, necessitating a frequent change in mailing addresses and phone numbers. The best source for recruitment has been bilingual notices, which are sent home by the classroom teachers, requesting information from interested families, and inviting parents to participate in the program. We ask parents to respond by returning a form to their child's teacher. Once we have this information, we invite families to an organizational meeting to explain the program. Other methods of recruitment have been community organizations and word of mouth from previous program participants.

For recruitment as well as retention purposes, we have found it useful to hire a community liaison at each site. Liaisons are usually bilingual individuals who are known and respected by the school and the parents. In Latino communities, females are more effective. Liaisons are instrumental in facilitating the entrance of program personnel into the community and in assessing the needs for the specific program in their school setting. With FLAME, they serve as a bridge between the families, the schools, and the university. Also, liaisons are able to identify people with the most needs and/or who are new in the community. In addition, if family patterns of attendance change, liaisons can talk to family members and inform program personnel about problems that could be addressed at this level. As a result, they have been an asset to the program in scheduling activities at the school and in contacting families when needed.

Supplemental Services

Besides childcare services for young children, and possibly for older children, FLAME offers other services that enhance the successful implementation of the program. For instance, transportation is a service that might be needed for some families, particularly in schools where children are bused and parents do not live in the community where the school is located. Sometimes we teach parents how to use public transportation and provide them with bus passes so they can attend classes. Parents who own a car might agree to bring other parents to the program. In return, we pay them a weekly fee for that service.

Occasionally, we also help parents complete job applications and, at times, this has been a topic for an ESL class. Also, as parents become friends with program staff, they begin asking questions about topics such as parental rights, child abuse, discipline, and the use of services at hospitals and banks. To fulfill the parents' need for this kind of information, we created the Summer Leadership Institute for FLAME participants. For the Institute, we invite speakers to talk to the parents about issues which are of interest to them, but which are not specifically related to literacy. For this activity, we bring all the parents to one site, usually a park district facility. To encourage their participation in the Institute, we offer free transportation from each school and also lunch. This activity provides networking opportunities and increases sharing of knowledge across FLAME sites. The Institutes have created a sense of community among all FLAME participants.

Role of School Teachers

Public schools are ideal settings for family literacy programs, or at least to make the connection with families. We have found that schools which serve as a FLAME site usually have better relationships between home and school and more communication between parents and teachers, even though classroom teachers are not involved in FLAME activities.

When we started talking to schools about FLAME in 1989, school principals were excited about having a family literacy program in their building. Their only concern was that we not use teachers' time. We agreed, but as the year progressed, teachers started asking FLAME personnel about the program. Some teachers noticed that FLAME parents seemed more involved with school activities, they responded promptly to teachers' requests, and they often sent the teacher a list of library books that their school-aged children had read that week.

Some teachers who realized the benefits of the program for participant families volunteered to help conduct scheduled FLAME workshops with parents about the home–school connection. They allowed parents to observe in their classrooms. They also agreed to meet with parents afterwards to answer their questions, deal with their concerns, and to share expectations. Through these experiences, teachers learned how much parents wanted to understand what happens in classrooms in the United States. They also learned that new immigrant Latino parents have very high expectations for their children. Parents talked about their children learning English and doing well in school; but they also discussed wanting their children to become, among other professions, lawyers, doctors, and teachers. Along with sharing information and ideas, teachers were able to confirm for parents their expectations that all children will succeed in their classrooms. The teachers who volunteered in these activities did not receive pay, but a gift of books for their classroom. These informal sessions lowered the anxiety that parents might have experienced when talking to teachers, and in turn teachers learned about the families and their hopes for their children.

Every year since then we have had teachers who volunteer for these workshops. We usually pay for substitute teachers to cover the classrooms while the teachers meet with parents. Principals have been supportive of the teachers' involvement as volunteers in Project FLAME.

Length of Participation in the Program

When we originally started working with families, we did not foresee a need to define a length of service to the families. Eventually, we learned that two years were needed to develop parents' competence and self-efficacy in supporting literacy learning at home. For example, emergent writing was a difficult concept to understand and accept. Most of the Latino parents in our program defined writing in terms of copying or penmanship, and they wanted their children to trace the words very clearly and neatly. It was not until the second year in the program that they started bringing samples of their children's emergent writing to show and discuss with their classmates. They also took two years to understand the need to ask different kinds of questions while sharing books with their children.

Parents who stayed more than two years began telling us that they were bored, and they wanted different activities, such as crafts, to be part of the program. We had to explain to those parents that the focus of the program was on early literacy and that they needed to graduate. This was not an easy step because the parents had developed networks, which they wanted to keep, but that were beyond the scope of our program.

Needs of Graduating Parents

It is very difficult to be involved with a group of families for two years and then graduate them. They have the expectation that you should tell them what to do next. Additionally, you feel some obligation to continue to support them. In the past, we have directed the majority of graduating parents to community organizations that offer ESL, technology, or sewing classes. We have been fortunate in that the communities where we worked had a variety of organizations, as well as very strong library and park district systems that were able to support FLAME graduates. Some parents have started discussion groups on various issues, meeting in different members' homes as a way to stay in touch. Another group discusses movies that they have watched together. Some of the FLAME personnel have been invited to these activities, and they have kept in contact with the families on their own.

Through the years, we also have created new modules for our program, which involve some graduating parents. The first was the Training of Trainers module, which was designed to develop capable leaders within the community who were qualified to offer the program once the university was no longer involved. To achieve this, each year two or three graduating parents per school are invited to become trainers of other parents. Those who are chosen demonstrate leadership skills, are good speakers, and are respected by other parents. They also understand the purpose of the program and are willing to commit to the longer training program. During their two years in the module, they meet with the university staff to plan literacy sessions with activities that are relevant and specific to their school and community. The first year, most of the trainers serve as teacher aides to the program. During the second year of training, they present workshops with the help of program staff. These parents are paid for the planning and teaching. Currently, some of the parents who graduated from this Training of Trainers module have been hired as family literacy teachers at schools that have adopted the FLAME model, while others have been hired by parent-oriented organizations as leaders in the community.

Many FLAME parents like to spend their free time volunteering in the school, and they find themselves in the classrooms, helping teachers. Teachers sometimes appreciate their help but do not have time to tell the parents exactly what to do. Because of this, we developed the

Parents as Volunteers module as part of FLAME. At the request of the principal or an individual teacher, we teach parents specific tasks that they can carry out in the classrooms. This module was very successful in a school where teachers told the FLAME staff specific objectives and activities to teach the parents before they went into the classroom.

In working with parents, it is very important for them to realize that you value and respect their cultural ways and their knowledge and that you want to support their goals beyond those related to their participation in your program. You have to make them aware that as they graduate from the program, they make room for new families who will benefit from the program as much as their own family.

Program Personnel

Personnel requirements for a program like FLAME vary depending on the setting. At the university, we rely on teaching assistants who are working toward teacher certification in a master's degree program. They teach ESL classes and literacy sessions, and help to coordinate activities. Through FLAME activities, they gain valuable experience in teaching literacy and in working with a diverse population. Since most teaching assistants are bilingual, working with the parents gives them an opportunity to practice their Spanish skills in a different environment.

Through the years I have learned what qualities to look for in teaching assistants for FLAME. Candidates who are successful with Latino parents are very accepting of cultural and linguistic differences. They must enjoy working with people in the community and show respect for the knowledge that parents bring to the learning situation. They appreciate the contributions of FLAME participants to the planning of sessions and workshops. Usually, they expect to learn a lot in the process, and they plan to use that knowledge when they become teachers.

School districts that have adopted the Project FLAME model across the country usually have different personnel arrangements than we do. In some schools, teachers provide the workshops as an after-school program. In other sites, teacher aides and parents are trained to implement the program. All of the personnel in these adaptations have received training about the program and its philosophy from qualified personnel from the university. We also use the Chicago program sites as demonstration centers for visitors who are considering adopting the model.

Issues of Change and Ethics

My work with families through Project FLAME has opened my eyes to issues of change in families as parents, mostly mothers, develop confidence, competence, and self-efficacy in their role as teachers for their children. Mothers talk about how they now plan activities for their children rather than allowing them to watch television. They mention their home literacy center and the books that the children borrow from the library. They also complain about the fact that they have to share the room where children do homework with their husband who is watching television. Sometimes they feel their husbands should get more involved in their children's learning and literacy activities and are successful in finding ways to include them. Other times, the father prefers that they move the literacy activities to another room while he watches television.

Situations like this one have created tension in some families. Some of these issues have been brought up in group discussions, and, together, we brainstorm possible solutions. It is important to find ways to deal with these issues without disturbing families' lives. The mothers are changing, they have more friends, they have networks of support, and they tend to spend more time outside their home. They have developed confidence in their role as teachers. This confidence enhances their self-efficacy, which affects other areas of their lives. How is this change impacting their family life? How does participation in a family literacy program affect the family? These are very important questions that need to be addressed by people working in family literacy.

Once change occurs in a community or a group, the issue of ethics of change comes into play. Change for what? Who changes? How does change affect people and communities? These issues need to be researched, but in the meantime they should not be overlooked.

Conclusion

In addition to program objectives and design, there are a number of supporting activities and components that could enhance the success of family literacy programs with culturally and linguistically different populations. The content and design of family literacy programs are very important to their success, but unless the program addresses the context and cultural concerns of the program participants, it might become irrelevant to the population to be served.

Community-based programs should be planned with an understanding of the context and culture of the prospective participants in the program. When deciding the content of the programs, developers need to recognize and respect the cultural models of learning and the discourses used by their participants. Examples include practices such as the role of storytelling in sharing literacy with children, who talks in the family, where they feel comfortable talking, and what can be asked. Likewise, in planning the time and place for the program, it is very important for Latinos that they have a say in the decision. Also, it is important to validate their knowledge and language. Family literacy programs should add to, rather than change, the repertoire of behaviors and practices used by parents to support their children's learning at home.

My experiences with Project FLAME, a family literacy program serving mostly Latino new immigrant families, has shown that flexibility in scheduling, attendance, and planned activities is one of the main characteristics of a successful program. Adapting the program to the participants' needs does not mean that the content, design, and focus of the program changes, but that input from participants is used to make the program more responsive to their needs. Families that feel their voices are heard by program staff often take ownership of the program and become more involved in all program activities. Opportunities for sharing personal and family knowledge and networking among participants enhance both attendance and active participation in training sessions. Allowing participants to discuss with each other ways in which they share literacy with their family demonstrates to program staff how the program content is affecting the parents' family literacy practices.

Since the concept of *"familia"* (Abi-Nader, 1991) is central in the lives of Latinos, a successful and relevant program for this population will include activities and services that meet the needs of different members of the family (e.g., children and grandparents), who in some capacity might participate in the program. In some situations, program policy needs to define who is considered family for inclusion in program activities.

The issues discussed in this chapter were not taken into account during the initial development and implementation of Project FLAME. They have been recognized and learned as a result of continued work with families. Program participants have been our best teachers in transforming a "functional" family literacy program (Rodríguez-Brown & Mulhern, 1993) into a program that parents own and use critically. To them, the Project FLAME staff owes "respeto" and gratitude.

Part III

The School-to-Home Connection

Introduction

Part I and Part II of this book deal with parental involvement and family literacy, especially as part of learning at home. Project FLAME is discussed as a family literacy program in which parents and children share knowledge in ways that are relevant to them and that also support their children's schooling. When working with parents who are culturally and/or linguistically diverse, family literacy programs ideally allow parents to expand their teaching repertoire to add new ways in which they share literacy with their children. Through these programs, parents learn about schooling in the United States and about ways in which they can support their children's learning. In this way, parents help to create a bridge between learning at home and learning at school.

However, the home–school connection is defined here as a two-way street. So far, the discussion has only involved parents and what they can do from their direction. This part of the book discusses the contributions that schools and teachers can make to complete the bridge that supports children's transition from home to school. Such a bridge is important for all children, but is especially relevant for children from families who are different from the mainstream and whose home knowledge base, culture, and discourses are different from those favored by U.S. schools.

These family differences represent potential obstacles for children from diverse communities. Teachers do not always realize that literacy practices are different or that they might hinder students' progress toward school literacy. According to McCarthey (1999), "The teachers' assumptions that students could make home–school connections on their own contributed to the literacy curriculum being more congruent with middle-class, home literacy experiences than working-class experiences" (p. 147). Children who grew up in environments where reading and writing of complex texts occurred frequently seemed to have more of a sense about writing and its conventions (Purcell-Gates, 1996).

Teale (1986) found that it was the use of literacy artifacts such as children's books that made a difference in children's literacy development. These observational studies show that evaluation of home backgrounds is complex since "print" is usually available in most homes, but it is difficult to describe how children, particularly those from diverse families, see literacy being used in their everyday lives.

Why is it important for congruency to exist between learning at home and at school? Several researchers believe that children whose discourses, culture, and knowledge are similar to those of the school seem to benefit the most from their school experiences (Purcell-Gates, 1996; Teale, 1986). When these factors are not similar, students usually struggle unless teachers realize the differences and take steps to mediate them. Contextualizing instruction is one thing teachers can do that motivates students to become more involved in their own learning. Tharp (as cited in Kyle, McIntyre, Miller, & Moore, 2002) believes that:

> Connecting teaching to who your students are can transform the bored student into an eager one, transform resentment into relationship, transform passivity into problem solving. But how can teachers know who their students are? Certainly by listening to them. And by listening to their parents.
>
> (p. viii)

When teachers and parents work together, they can develop some continuity that provides students with clear goals and the assistance necessary to succeed in school. Teachers should find ways to connect with knowledge from the community and the families. This facilitates children's transition from home to school, and can also make the curriculum more relevant for all children. The following pages describe ways in which some teachers have learned about the effectiveness of building connections with parents and communities, and how they practice the school-to-home connection.

Chapter 7

Ways to Connect with Community and Home Knowledge

Introduction

Some teachers think that holding semi-annual, parent-teacher conferences and sending home a monthly calendar are all that is needed to maintain some kind of home–school connection. Others put more effort into class newsletters or homework forms that must be signed by the parent. Although these activities ask parents to be more involved in their children's education, they do not provide much opportunity for parents to exchange information about the family itself or for teachers to share the expectations of the school. The ideas presented in this chapter involve teachers to a much greater extent and with much greater results.

Teacher Training Programs

The Funds of Knowledge Project

Working with Vygotsky's ideas about how cultural practices and resources mediate the development of thinking, Gonzalez et al. (1993) developed a procedure for classroom teachers to learn about existing "funds of knowledge" in their school community. This term refers to knowledge, skills, and traits that parents or a community possess. Members of the community share with each other and with their children, so the transfer of knowledge is intergenerational. Once teachers learn about the knowledge that exists in the community and their students' homes, they find ways to use that knowledge to inform their curriculum. In doing so, they make schooling more relevant for children from the community since they can apply what they have learned at home to school learning situations. Since their inception several years ago, the Funds of Knowledge study groups have become a pedagogical model of teacher training in which teachers learn to theorize about household knowledge and practices.

The concept of funds of knowledge, as developed by Vélez-Ibañez and Greenberg (1992), is based on the proposition that understanding the knowledge that children acquire at home and the context in which that knowledge is acquired is necessary to "understand the construction of cultural identity and the emergence of a cultural personality" (p. 336). This cultural identity then supports learning in a school setting. Their work has been done with a U.S.-Mexican population whose identities Vélez-Ibañez and Greenberg believe are not represented in educational structures and practices. This lack of representation leads to what the researchers call a "deficiency model" of instruction for minority students.

Gonzalez, Moll, and Amanti (2005) described the Funds of Knowledge Project, including study groups in which teachers are trained to transform their teaching by making the curriculum more contextualized to the students and their communities. In the process of investigating community knowledge, teachers learn to be ethnographers. They visit households and collect information, which they later share in group meetings. As teachers discuss their experiences with home visits, they theorize about the meaning of the funds of knowledge found in the community, and they share ideas about how to connect schools to children's lives. The group environment is supportive and non-judgmental, and participants can safely become risk-takers.

Within other study group activities, theory and practice are studied in a dual manner. However, it is not always theory informing practice; household knowledge and practices, as reported by the teachers, are also the object of theorizing. As household knowledge is theorized, it is discussed within the context of the school curriculum. As a result, participant teachers are able to connect families' funds of knowledge to part of their curriculum as thematic units.

Teachers use field notes and artifacts as well as journal and academic articles as they collect data, theorize, and try to understand household practices as a "partial representation of reality" (Gonzalez et al., 2005, p. 21). The funds of knowledge that are uncovered become "cultural artifacts" that help the teachers mediate their understanding of the social lives of the households studied. It is these artifacts that transform teachers' opinions about resources that can be found in the communities where their students live.

According to Gonzalez et al., "the 'funds of knowledge' of a community are not a laundry list of immutable cultural traits, but rather are historically contingent, emergent within relations of power, and not necessarily equally distributed" (p. 25). In other words, knowledge changes with the times, and those with more power might also have more knowledge. Vélez-Ibañez and Greenberg (1992) believe that funds of knowledge as social capital are not only received from others but they can also be modified or produced in relation to different circumstances. Teachers can modify or adapt what they have learned from the households and then integrate this new knowledge into classroom activities. With the teacher as mediator, students use the new knowledge and activities to inquire and learn in school in ways that are relevant to them.

Teachers who have participated in Funds of Knowledge study groups view themselves as teacher researchers. They report on how the newly acquired skills have transformed their instructional practice by making the curriculum and the general school experience more relevant for children who are culturally and linguistically different. They have learned how to observe domains of knowledge, interaction patterns, cultural practices, and discourses found in the communities where they work. All this information has allowed them to become mediators, not only for the children in their classrooms but also between the school and the home. These teachers see culturally and linguistically different families as "resourceful, connected and full of life experiences" (Tenery, 2005, p. 129). They have created instructional spaces in their classrooms where children, language, and culture are immersed with the teacher's goals and the school's curricular requirements, in order to make schooling more relevant for the students. Teachers who have completed Funds of Knowledge training consider themselves mediators between the home and school and, as such, are real contributors to the home–school connection.

Amanti (2005), a participant in the project, states that she has learned that culture is not static, and she "has gained an appreciation for the complexity and the importance of understanding how the idea of culture has been contested and transformed" (p. 131). She explains how the purpose of the Funds of Knowledge training "is not about replicating what students have learned at home, but about using students' knowledge and prior experiences as a scaffold for new learning" (p. 135). Amanti finds that knowing about students' prior knowledge facilitates the planning of instruction and helps her avoid teaching what students already know. For Amanti, the study and application of funds of knowledge is an important piece that is missing in education today.

Another teacher (Hensley, 2005) in the Funds of Knowledge project reports learning how to use specific children's interests to motivate their school learning possibilities. The experience has changed her relationship with parents and children who are culturally different. She believes:

If teachers include parents and families in the formula for educating children and seriously listen to and value their funds of knowledge, we will turn the key that unlocks the door to a bright future for children and their parents.

(p. 150)

Browning-Aiken (2005), also a graduate of the project, feels that the training in funds of knowledge and the families that she studied became "educational resources for curriculum development and provide insight into more effective educational practice" (p. 167). She relates how she applies her understanding about the funds of knowledge that she found in the families of her students to develop a thematic module on Border Connections, using the concepts of *educación* (education) and networking across borders. For Browning-Aiken, the availability of cultural knowledge and local resources proves very useful when appropriate textbooks and library materials are limited.

Moll (2005) believes that the Funds of Knowledge Project encourages parents from participant families, especially mothers, to develop relationships of "confianza" with the teachers. This Spanish word indicates a reciprocal relationship of help when needed and trust that is based on friendship. Such a relationship with a teacher creates opportunities for parents to build relationships with the school and also learn about the process of schooling in the United States. This relationship also can become reciprocal between parents and teachers, acting as a bridge that supports the children's learning. The funds of knowledge discovered by teachers are an authentic, bidirectional, home–school connection and one that should be in existence in all classrooms, particularly in classrooms with large numbers of children who are culturally and linguistically different.

Family Visits

Using similar principles as the Funds of Knowledge Project, Kyle and McIntyre (2000) created a model of family visits as a way to establish and enhance communication between teachers and parents in order to support students' learning. As teacher-researchers, the authors visited homes of students. The home visits indirectly had an effect on the relationships between parents and children who were visited by the teachers. The authors believed that the home visits allowed children to realize how much knowledge their parents had and could share with their teachers. Children saw their teachers respecting that knowledge, so they tended to appreciate and respect their parents more. Parents also saw themselves as respected experts about their children and were very willing to share information with the teachers.

The home visits helped teachers learn more about their students' outside interests, families, and home routines. Although this particular project does not show how the home visits impacted instruction, opening communication with parents is a tool that facilitates the connection between home and school, which is always beneficial to children's learning. Kyle and McIntyre's research has resulted in a book and several articles that are now used for teacher training.

Out-of-School Programs

Out-of-school literacy learning can contribute to the literacy development of children who are culturally and linguistically different. Some programs can reach reluctant or unmotivated students that classroom teachers cannot. Although young students might struggle to adjust and be successful in the different literacy environment of the mainstream school, older students begin to realize that what they are expected to learn is not relevant to their home lives. They also realize that what they learned at home does not seem to count at school. In fact, there exists a body of research that shows the frustration that children and families suffer when the knowledge that children have learned at home and in the community is not recognized at school (Cushman, 1998; Rogers, 2001; Skilton-Sylvester, 2002). There are also studies that show the contributions that out-of-school programs and community organizations make in creating alternative bridges to literacy. These activities are sensitive to and support the development of children who are frustrated or who feel that school is not relevant to them (Gutiérrez, Baquedano-López, Alvarez, & Chiu, 1999; Heath & McLaughlin, 1993; Knobel, 1999).

An out-of-school program that has been used with African American and Latino children is The Fifth Dimension. Cole and Griffin (1986) originally developed this program as an out-of-school club. The main activity structure is based on play and communication, whereby children interact with a Wizard of unknown gender and age. The Wizard sends e-mail messages to participant children, showing an interest in what is happening in their lives. The Wizard also receives complaints and requests from the children who learn to write messages on the computer in order to communicate with the Wizard. This activity is an ideal tool to give children an authentic purpose for developing writing skills outside the school setting.

Gutiérrez et al. (1999) have used the Wizard in an out-of-school setting with Latino children, calling it La Maga. The activity familiarizes children with Las Redes (The Net). Since the program is bilingual, children can choose the topic and the language they use when they write to La Maga. Gutiérrez et al. believe that this activity allows bilingual children to show "bilingual, bicultural and biliterate knowledge and skills" (p. 91) in a relevant and low anxiety environment.

Martha, one of the participants in the program, showed increased proficiency in both Spanish and English, and sophistication in the use of both languages and registers as she developed her literacy skills. Gutiérrez and her colleagues believe that contexts such as the one provided in this activity allow for hybrid language use to flourish, as children create a "third space" (Gutiérrez, Baquedano-López, & Tejeda, 1999) using both alternative and dominant discourses. They believe that the La Maga context is a supplement to school that allows participants to show how much they know, even when they are not performing well in school.

The types of out-of-school activities described above, although many times unrelated to the school curriculum and the teachers' expectations, encourage children to develop literacy skills in playful settings that do not resemble school. Such settings seem to support learning for children who might feel alienated and dissatisfied with the school curriculum. Programs such as the Wizard can be considered part of the home–school connection. They are community-based, they provide learning structures relevant to the children, and they value the knowledge and culture that children bring to the learning situation.

Missed Opportunities

It is the teacher's lack of understanding of cultural differences that many times alienates children from learning at school. The following example puts a name to a culturally and linguistically different child, an Indochinese girl, and illustrates the results of failing to connect with the home and failing to learn more about the culture of the students in the classroom. Skilton-Sylvester (2002) describes the case of a Cambodian girl, Nam, who was literate at home but not at school. Nam's family members were refugees from Cambodia where formal education for girls was not valued. According to Skilton-Sylvester, Nam did not see herself as bicultural; she thought her academic limitations were a consequence of being Cambodian. Within the climate of the school that Nam attended, it was not cool to be seen reading books. The peer culture, as well as the school academic program, overlooked students' interests and living experiences, and students' development as readers and writers was not supported. School literacy activities included filling in the blanks, completing worksheets, and copying from already existing texts. Many of the activities which Nam and the other girls in the study would have valued, such as writing journals and autobiographies or drawing, were not considered part of the school curriculum. Skilton-Sylvester found that, in spite of this, the girls enjoyed an active writing life at home, which was not visible at school.

Although Nam was a prolific writer at home, her writing was imbedded in visual images, which were not accepted and valued at school. According to Skilton-Sylvester:

> If students' lives only enter the school walls through writing that is on the periphery of how students are ultimately evaluated, we have not created the bridge needed to make the out-of-school strengths of a student such as Nam visible when she is tackling academic literacy ... Bridges need to be built between these multisensory

messages and the ways that school writing is often judged and inter-
preted based on the messages that the words themselves convey.

(p. 85)

Skilton-Sylvester (2002) felt that Nam believed in the value of the
written word to make meaning and connect with others. This belief was
reflected in her continued efforts to write at home. For her, schools and
teachers need to find a foundation for school literacy which accepts and
understands not only the words but also the world of culturally different children as they try to engage these children in new words and a
new world that exists at school, the academic discourse. Skilton-
Sylvester believes that "We, as teachers, have as much to learn from
Nam as she from us" (p. 88). In the case of Nam, in spite of the lack of
an out-of-school program that would support her interest in writing,
she was pursuing that interest at home but her efforts were not recognized at school. Of three possible resources—school, community
organizations, and family—none were supportive of her literacy development. This example is an illustration of what can occur when
teachers are not aware that culturally and linguistically different children might bring to school cultural ways of learning and discourses
which are not congruent with the ways learning occurs in schools
developed for a mainstream population.

Conclusion

The Funds of Knowledge study groups (Gonzalez et al., 2005) and
Family Visits (Kyle & McIntyre, 2000) are two formal and organized
programs to help teachers learn to connect with the parents and
community of the students who are in their classrooms. The knowledge
that teachers gain from such connections can then be integrated into the
curriculum, making instruction more interesting and familiar for the
students. There should be many more efforts by universities with
teacher preparation programs to inform teacher candidates of the
wealth of knowledge that exists in the communities and ways to incorporate it into their instruction.

Out-of-school programs also represent an opportunity to involve
community organizations in literacy activities that might engage frustrated or reluctant learners. Some programs, especially those that meet
in a public school and hire teachers from the school, function simply as
an extension of the school day by providing more practice in regular
schoolwork. Programs like La Maga have been adapted for the
community in which they exist and for the students who attend their
sessions. Adequate funding and training of personnel are needed for
more programs like this to increase.

Chapter 8

Teachers Making Connections

Introduction

There are a number of ways in which teachers can individually make connections with the home and community. This chapter looks at four different teachers who found a way to successfully bring parents' knowledge into the classroom and, in some cases, to share school practices with parents. None of the teachers had attended classes or been in projects that emphasized the need or advantages of making connections with parents. Yet all were able to learn more about parents, their attitudes, and their knowledge.

Teaching Style

Dyson (2003) described a group of first-grade children, who called themselves the Brothers and Sisters, as they followed different paths toward becoming writers. While one group of boys used their love and knowledge of sports as an enticement to writing, a group of girls took advantage of their knowledge about African American singers to write and sing their own songs. Their writing was not conventional, and they were not receiving conventional instruction in writing, because Rita, their teacher, saw benefits in allowing children to follow alternate pathways to literacy, particularly in the arts. Rita (a pseudonym) was also very accepting of the knowledge that students bring from home and the community, and, as reported by Dyson, the children found opportunities to use their cultural knowledge to acquire academic skills.

It was interesting the way Rita valued cultural differences in her classroom. In a diverse society, where children bring different home literacy experiences to school, Rita was very effective. Dyson (2003) described Rita, who was trained in England, as:

> A highly experienced teacher with an expansive curriculum and a critical, reflective disposition. Her efforts were also enfolded within

a structured institution, the school, which is oriented toward the societal mainstream and which continues to be under enormous pressure to narrow the curriculum and the possible negotiating room for children and teachers.

(p. 27)

Rita was also described as "a visual artist and a music lover. She was serious about engaging the children in a careful study of visual artists and in their own thoughtful production of artistic works" (p. 19). During the time when she was a teacher in England and later in the United States, Rita valued the relationship between the arts and learning "the basics," and she believed it is possible to teach the basics through art. Dyson explained Rita's vision of children as decision makers who are critically involved with the world around them. She believed her role as a teacher was one of helping children learn how to learn, rather than one of directly teaching basic skills (ABCs, numbers, writing sentences) as required by the state where she worked.

Although Rita's style of teaching was problematic in light of the school curriculum, which called for the teaching of basics organized in a sequential manner (sound/symbol relations, sentences, genres), her students reacted positively to her teaching style. They brought media texts from home (movies, cartoons, songs) as resources that, although symbolic and textual, were not sequentially related. Rita respected her students' knowledge and experiences with the media texts. The children also learned about the arts through traditional texts and artifacts, which were chosen for their cultural relevance. Rita viewed the children's involvement in the arts as a resource to help them learn, which could then fulfill the requirements of the mandated school curriculum.

It could be interesting to find out whether it was Rita's English training that led her to respect and accept children's out-of-school knowledge and interest as a tool to motivate children to learn at school, or whether she learned to do so as she became an experienced teacher. In today's educational climate, a teacher like Rita can serve as an example for teachers who work in classrooms with diverse learners. Through her teaching style and respect for community and home knowledge, she was supporting the transition of her students from home to school. By providing learning opportunities that were relevant to the children, she indirectly led them to learn what was required by the school curriculum.

Classroom Routines

Wonderful Wednesdays

Caltha Crowe is an experienced third-grade teacher who believes that the home–school connection is a two-way street. In an effort to inform parents about how their children learn in her classroom and as a way for her to become acquainted with the parents, she created an activity that she calls Wonderful Wednesdays (Crowe, 2004). This activity occurs weekly or biweekly, and all parents are invited to visit the classroom any time during the school day. In order to accommodate her visitors, Crowe plans classroom activities such as workshops, which allows parents to participate in a variety of activities with their child. Parents are free to spend as much time as they want in the classroom, but they are to be full participants in all activities, not passive observers.

Crowe realizes that what children learn and do in school today is quite different from what their parents experienced when they attended school. Through classroom visits, parents acquire a more realistic view of the learning environment. Children learn through different kinds of activities or class routines, such as workshops, group projects, discussion groups, and games, as well as more academic, direct teaching activities. Through Wonderful Wednesdays, Crowe hopes that parents will understand the variety of approaches that can be used for instruction, as well as the nature of low-stress and high-rigor activities involved in learning throughout a school day.

Wonderful Wednesdays also allows Crowe to learn about the parents of her students. She feels that it is helpful for her to become acquainted with the parents just as it is important for the parents to learn about her classroom and teaching approach. Because she teaches in a large school in a busy neighborhood, it is difficult for parents to find time to establish close connections. However, Crowe feels, "This connection not only makes my work more enjoyable, but it is essential to my work, for in order to teach my students well, I need to know something of their life outside the school" (p. 2).

Connections made through Wonderful Wednesdays have enabled Crowe to set up conferences and discussions with parents about their child's needs and about specific ways in which they can support their child's learning at home. Crowe feels that participation in classroom activities allows parents to be more relaxed when meeting with her, especially during more formal school activities, such as report card day or conferences. Wonderful Wednesdays have also provided opportunities to create a sense of community, not only among students in the classroom, but with their families.

This activity is especially appealing for parents of children who are culturally and linguistically different. Since the classroom is open to all parents with no specific time commitments, they might feel more accepted and at ease while visiting. Linguistically and culturally different parents are usually very curious about schools in the United States. They want to find out what goes on in classrooms, and through an activity such as Wonderful Wednesdays, they will feel welcomed and wanted in their child's classroom, and less anxious about meeting the teacher who invited them to visit.

For teachers, the presence of parents in the classroom is an excellent opportunity to learn more about them, about funds of knowledge existing in the homes, and about resources that could be used in the classroom to make the curriculum more relevant to all children.

Book Talk and Literacy Learning

Karen Bean had been using silent sustained reading (SSR) in her fourth-grade classroom for years. In order to make this activity more effective and to fulfill requirements of the state learning standards in listening and speaking, Bean (2006) developed an activity that she calls Book Talk. During SSR, students choose their own books and read silently during the first 20 minutes of the school day, while Bean checks attendance and homework that students have returned. When students finish reading their book, they prepare to talk about it to the rest of the class. Using forms with prompt questions that serve as scaffolding, students write a summary, choose a vocabulary word to share, and select a favorite short passage to read aloud. Then they practice for their presentation.

When it is their turn to do a Book Talk, students have three minutes to discuss the book they read. Then they field questions from their classmates. The questioning session, which usually lasts from three to five minutes, is also scaffolded and modeled to help students develop listening skills, learn to ask critical questions, extend the reader's discussion, and deepen understanding of issues and events in the book. Book Talk takes place every day. The rotation allows each student to present six Book Talks in a school year.

"Book Talk" is an activity setting (Cambourne, 2001) that allows children to increase comprehension and fluency during SSR, practice listening and speaking skills, and participate in interactive learning. According to Bean (2006), "The Book Talk activity setting extends the SSR portion of the school day by adding social interaction and an opportunity for independent practice with a broader range of literacy skills and behaviors" (p. 2). As students become more familiar with the Book Talk activity setting, they learn how to use oral language in a more meaningful way and in the process engage in different "school-based literacy tasks" (p. 6).

The "Book Talk" activity is sociocultural in nature and was planned to be so. Bean realized that not all of her students came from the same home environment, brought the same literacy experiences to the classroom, or even spoke the same language. Some of them had learned at home the same literacy discourse that is used in schools, but others had not. They must learn a secondary discourse, the academic discourse used in school. Bean's understanding of her students, along with her sociocultural perspective, resulted in the various forms of scaffolding and modeling that are part of Book Talk and that support students in learning and practicing the school discourse, especially for the first few presentations.

According to Bean (2006), "a sociocultural perspective of literacy learning suggests that all children, regardless of their language backgrounds, need opportunities to observe others who use and are also learning more about this secondary, school based discourse" (p. 6). Through the Book Talk process, children "are provided with an opportunity to acquire the discourse used at school in a way that closely resembles the interactive and assisted performance learning that supports children outside of school" (p. 3). This sociocultural view is supported by results of research conducted by Cazden (1988), Gee (1989), Heath (1983, 1986), and Rogoff (1990).

How does this activity represent a school-to-home connection? As Bean developed and refined Book Talk as an activity setting in her classroom, she decided to videotape the students' presentations. Students took the videotape home and watched it with their parents. Both child and parents were asked to complete a response form afterwards, which was returned to the teacher. The videotapes gave children the opportunity to see themselves as they presented their book talks, reflect on their performance, and make plans for improvement in subsequent book talks. Parents also had the opportunity to see their own child perform and to understand the kinds of activities and learning that were taking place in their child's classroom.

The videotapes were originally intended as a keepsake for parents, many of them from different cultural backgrounds, but their written responses and verbal comments to Bean showed her that watching the tape had unexpected consequences. Many parents were surprised at the ways in which their children were learning at school. They commented on the degree of sophistication and poise that some students exhibited during their presentation, and reflected on the value of the Book Talk activity setting as a learning tool that will support their child in the future.

After watching the first tape, parents became more involved with their child's preparation for subsequent Book Talk presentations, supporting their child in different ways. Some helped children practice their oral presentation, while others made suggestions about the content of the presentation or its delivery. Others asked a variety of questions so their child would be prepared to answer any questions that their class-mates might ask. In many ways parents were using their own cultural ways of learning while supporting their children's learning.

Over the course of a school year, Bean observed her students becoming more confident and competent participants in all aspects of Book Talk. In order to document the kinds of learning that were taking place and to evaluate the effectiveness of the scaffolding and modeling, Bean conducted a qualitative study of the activity setting (2006). She found reciprocal and interactive influences within all aspects of Book Talk and among all forms of scaffolding. What was surprising was the influence that parents had on the presentations of other students in the class-room, not just their own child. Once they learned what was required of their child during a Book Talk, they were able to use their own personal knowledge to support and scaffold their child's literacy progress. Students who mentioned their parents' help or suggestions during their oral presentation shared this knowledge with all of the students in the class-room. The influence of this parental knowledge was evident when other students made use of it in later presentations. Parents became partners in their children's learning and, in doing so, they helped create a bridge between learning at home and at school.

Connecting Through Homework

Laura Arroyo taught ESL classes at a predominantly African American school in a large city in the Midwest (Arroyo, 2003). Latino students from all grade levels were bused to her school from other communities so they could receive instruction in English. Since the school was not in the community where the children lived, and the parents did not have easy access to the school, Arroyo looked for ways to connect with the parents and to use their knowledge in her instructional activities. She designed a survey to investigate parents' views of their role as teacher for their children and their involvement with school homework. On report card day, parents were asked to complete the 25 questions on the survey. Some questions asked for demographic information, such as country of origin and parents' language proficiency in both Spanish and English. Other questions asked parents about their attitudes toward homework (Do you agree that daily homework is important for your child? Who helps your child when he/she does homework?), or about family homework routines (Is the television on while your children do homework? Do they do homework in the same place and at the same time? Can you usually help your child with homework? What are some of the reasons why you cannot help?).

Finally, Arroyo asked parents about their role in educating (*educar*) versus their role in teaching (*enseñar*) their children. This was done to determine whether this dichotomy that is widely reported in research with Latino families (Reese & Gallimore, 2000; Rodríguez-Brown, 2001a, 2001b) was present among the parents of her students.

Some of the results were revealing. For example, Arroyo assumed that parents from small towns and "ranchos" had less education and, therefore, would have children who were experiencing more difficulty with schoolwork. She was surprised to find that the parents of her best students came from rural areas in Mexico.

Most of the parents reported very low oral and reading proficiency in English. The same parents (over 90%) reported high proficiency in both reading and writing in Spanish. This was revealing to the teacher, who had expected parents to report low levels of writing ability. This assumption was based on samples of parents' writing, which she had in her classroom. She also thought that parents' low levels of literacy in English were sometimes the reason why parents seldom visited the school.

In response to questions about homework, parents felt that homework was very important for their children's learning, and they thought daily homework was necessary. The same parents reported that they often or sometimes helped their children with homework, but mothers were the most involved with children's homework. On questions about homework routines, 74% of the parents said their children did not or very seldom watched television while doing homework. Eighty-seven percent of the parents stated that their children were assigned a regular time and place to complete their homework.

Only 25% of the parents said they often helped their children with homework. The reasons given were lack of English proficiency (67%), lack of clarity of the assignments (38%), and lack of knowledge of content (19%). Ninety-four percent of the parents reported difficulty in talking to their child's teacher. This was due to lack of English proficiency (87%) and lack of knowledge about how to ask the teacher questions (20%).

When asked what they did to support their children's learning, 93% of parents transported their children to and from school, 46% attended regularly scheduled parent-teacher conferences, and 33% had informal conversations with teachers and volunteered as field trip chaperones. Only 20% reported taking their children to the library.

When asked questions regarding the "educar" (to educate) and "enseñar" (to teach) dichotomy, parents confirmed the previous findings reported in the research literature. Most parents related the word "educar" to the teaching of morals and values and saw that as their responsibility, while they defined "to teach" as "what they teach at school" (book knowledge).

The results of her 2003 survey helped Arroyo learn more about the parents, their attitudes toward her school, and their homework practices. She learned that these parents really cared about their children's schooling and well-being. Sometimes, they checked that the children completed their homework, but they could not revise the content of the homework, due to lack of English proficiency and/or schooling.

Arroyo feels she has benefited from what she learned about the community in which her students live. Now she is trying to find ways to connect parents with the school so they can learn more about what happens in their children's classrooms and be more involved in their children's education. Her initial suggestion that the school offer after-school ESL classes for parents was ignored. More recently, with a new principal at the school and with support from the district's central office, she is planning to start an ESL program for Latino parents. She hopes this activity will enhance parent participation in school activities and lead to greater parental involvement with homework.

Arroyo also has learned about the Funds of Knowledge project (Gonzalez et al., 2005) being used by teachers in Arizona and believes that home visits could allow her to know more about the families' knowledge. Currently, she is thinking about ways to integrate the acquired knowledge into her ESL curriculum. Then she can provide relevant activities for her students during the 45 minutes of each day that they spend with her.

The school-home connection, Arroyo believes, is necessary in order to help parents understand their expected role in U.S. schools, in learning about schooling in the United States, and in learning English as a way to support their children's learning. Right now, she knows that the main home-to-school connection parents make is "to educate" their children to be good citizens. She thinks parents also should be able "to teach" their children, and she sees her role as one of helping parents learn how to support their children's learning at home. For now, she thinks the ESL classes will be just a beginning step toward a more comprehensive program to help parents develop a bridge between home and school.

Summary

Working with a variety of cultures and languages, these teachers each found a way to establish or broaden the bridge between home and school, to use parents' knowledge to augment students' learning in class, or both. One brought parents to the classroom, while another sent the classroom home to the parents in the form of videotapes. One learned much about parents' differences, and another showed respect for and awareness of her students' cultural differences. The teachers' activities were unique to their particular school, classroom, and cultural setting, but all were effective in conveying to parents the teacher's acceptance and appreciation for the knowledge the parents already have, as well as their involvement in their child's literacy instruction. Once teachers have made these kinds of connections with their students' parents, they will find it easier to continue to do so with future classrooms of students.

Chapter 9

Teaching Teachers

Introduction

In the fall of 2003, I taught a graduate seminar for teachers on the topic of in-school and out-of-school learning. The purposes of the class were to raise teachers' awareness of the knowledge that culturally and linguistically different children might bring from home, and to show them how this knowledge could be used to support learning at school. In the process, we had many questions. Why is it that culturally different children are many times uninterested or bored in school? What can schools, and especially teachers, do to make school learning and classroom activities more relevant and interesting to all children?

We also learned about the role that out-of-school programs and community organizations have in supporting literacy learning and in making connections with the home and sometimes with the school. We discussed the characteristics of these types of programs, the relevance of their curriculum to children's lives, and how they accepted the children's knowledge and used it as a steppingstone to new learning in ways that did not resemble school learning.

Through class readings and discussion we learned about such efforts as the Funds of Knowledge study groups being offered at the University of Arizona (Moll et al., 1992). We debated the feasibility of visiting homes and collecting ethnographic data to learn about community knowledge in a large city. We discussed ways in which parents' knowledge might be seen as a resource that could be used to enrich and contextualize the school curriculum.

We also read Dyson's work (2003) and spent time discussing Rita, the teacher in the Brothers and Sisters classroom described by Dyson. Questions that were raised and answered reflected a wide range of concerns for these experienced teachers. Was she teaching the content required by the school? Were the students learning to read and write? Why were they having fun while learning? What were the qualities that Rita had as a teacher that made her respect the knowledge that the children brought from home and the community? Was she developing some continuity between home and school? Was she really fostering the creation of a bridge between home and school? Was this bridge supporting children's literacy learning and development?

As part of the class requirements, students wrote a research paper and/or developed a classroom activity that dealt with some aspect of the school curriculum for their grade level and that made a school-to-home connection. In the following pages, I describe the work of two teachers from the class. These women had different backgrounds and experiences. One was a Latino, bilingual kindergarten teacher who lived in a neighborhood close to the school. The other was a monolingual, European American, sixth-grade teacher who did not live in the neighborhood but had many years of teaching experience with bilingual students. However, both worked in schools where the student population was over 95% Latino. Both teachers knew and respected the communities where they worked, and both respected the diversity and cultural differences within the student population. Their projects illustrate how teachers can follow the required school curriculum while planning well-structured activities that include community resources to make the curriculum culturally relevant, use community knowledge to increase school learning, and make school more interesting to the children.

The Teacher of the Day Project

This particular project took place in a kindergarten bilingual classroom in a school where over 90% of the children were Mexican or Mexican-American. Jackie Medina, the teacher, wanted to connect with her students' parents to make them feel welcome at school (Medina, 2003). She also hoped that parents would come to realize that teachers are not the only ones responsible for their children's learning and that, regardless of their level of education, parents can contribute to their child's learning by using their own talents or knowledge, even if it is not school-related. She saw her role of teacher as supporting parents in recognizing the funds of knowledge that existed in their homes and community, which could help their children learn and succeed in school. Citing Ada and Zubizarreta (2001), Medina expressed her belief that teachers should enrich their curriculum by creating culturally relevant relationships with their students' parents and the school community.

Description of the Project

Medina created an activity setting in which parents were invited to become Teacher of the Day in her classroom. Parents who volunteered were to use their own talents and knowledge, as well as their own cultural ways to plan an activity and then share it with her students. First, she sent a letter home that explained the project to the parents and described some possible activities they could use in the classroom if they were to participate in the Teacher for a Day activity. She also sent a survey asking parents to identify their talents and inviting them to consider being a part of the project.

Six parents, all mothers, agreed to participate. Medina identified the parent-teachers by the activity that they shared with the class. They were the reader, the puppet-maker, the chef, the craft teacher, the dance instructor, and the game organizer. All of them made their own plans and prepared the materials needed for the activities or lesson they were teaching. Since some parents were nervous about their role as teachers, their own children were chosen as their assistants during the activity.

The children in the classroom were very excited about, and full of anticipation, for the Teacher for a Day activity every Friday. They were respectful of their "Friday Teachers" and asked many relevant questions. The child whose mother was the next Teacher for a Day felt very proud and was permitted to give the other students clues about the special activity to take place the following Friday. This activity replaced "Free Center Time" on Fridays, and the children were very willing to change their routine.

Lessons Learned

As part of her project, Medina collected field notes and also asked the participating mothers to complete a questionnaire about the activity. She was surprised by the parents' insightfulness when they identified specific content that they hoped students had learned through their activities. For example, the reader wanted the children to learn the names of different animals, while the game organizer expected the children to recall information, such as the letters used in her game.

The mothers also reflected on their classroom management skills, their effectiveness as a teacher, the problems they encountered as teachers, and the need for patience in teachers. They commented on ways to improve their instruction, such as having more student involvement. Mothers expressed surprise with the engagement of the students and commented on the children's eagerness to learn.

From the field notes, Medina learned that her students were more involved and on-task when the parents' activities resembled school-like activities. In less structured activities such as crafts, they were more relaxed and seemed to be having fun. Medina was surprised at how well her young students adapted to the different social contexts for learning that were created by each different parent-as-teacher activity (i.e., reading, cooking, or dancing).

Parents enjoyed the activity immensely, and many of them asked to be invited again, once all parents were given the opportunity to participate. Mothers who were nervous at the beginning of their activity appeared to relax once they discovered that they were able to teach and engage students. These mothers also were more willing to visit the classroom and talk to the teacher during the school year than those who were not part of the project. Medina (2003) explained how she intends to continue this school-to-home activity in future years. She also hopes that some fathers will be able to participate.

Through this Teacher for a Day activity, Medina learned how parents can become important resources for school learning while using materials and activities that are culturally relevant for the students, and she hopes that other teachers learn how to "tap into those funds of knowledge" (p. 12) available in family homes and in the community.

Once teachers like Medina learn about parents' knowledge, which may be very different from what is in the school curriculum, and find ways to include it in their curriculum, they also realize the value of making connections between the school and the home. They understand that the home–school connection is a two-way street, and that teachers have a responsibility as well as the parents. It is important for parents to support children's learning at home as a bridge that helps the children's transition between home and school, but that bridge will be stronger if teachers find ways to use parents' and community knowledge to make school more relevant to children in diverse classrooms.

Shakespeare in Pilsen

The second project was developed by Andrea Lancer (2005) in her sixth-grade classroom. As a teacher in a Latino neighborhood school in Chicago, Lancer respected her students' language and culture. She also had high expectations for all her students, in spite of the fact that only 20% tested at/or above grade level in reading.

Although in many schools minority students are marginalized or isolated, Lancer's students were considered the mainstream, since over 95% of the school population was Latino, mostly of Mexican American background. Still, she felt that her students were "not inspired to achieve academically" (p. 48).

Through her readings for the class at the university, Lancer learned that sometimes literacy is defined only in terms of language and communication practices that occur in school. This ideological bias, reported by Hull and Schultz (2002), exists to the detriment of low-income and minority students who are judged deficient on the basis of test results. Hull and Schultz believed that many minority and culturally different students engage in out-of-school literacy practices, such as using technology or reading manuals, activities that are not valued or even recognized by schools. They felt that if schools and teachers were to acknowledge and value those skills, they could use them as connections to school practices. Lancer stated that "if teachers were willing to investigate the alternative literacies of students and incorporate them into the school environment, these literacies could serve as a link to most in-school literacy tasks" (p. 47). With this understanding in mind, and as part of her class project, she decided to teach her students a play written by Shakespeare in a way that allowed them to apply their out-of-school literacy and relate the play to their own lives.

Using Drama to Enhance Literacy Learning

As a teacher who loves the arts and one who likes to integrate subjects to strengthen the curriculum, Lancer decided to teach a Shakespearean play during her literacy instruction and integrate it with the study of Shakespeare and of Renaissance Europe that was part of her sixth-grade curriculum. She hoped that reading Shakespeare would carry some status for her sixth graders, since his plays are usually studied by older students. She chose *Romeo and Juliet* because she thought that most of her students already knew something about the play. Also, she felt that sixth graders could relate to the elements of romance in the play. Lancer (2005) reported her belief that "high quality material produces high quality response, and programs that promote an enriched, high-expectation curriculum have been shown to be very effective for students like mine" (p. 47).

According to Lancer, drama is an under-used tool in the literacy classroom. Watching different versions of a play and discussing multiple interpretations of a role help students understand the ideas and emotional state of the playwright. Although she knew that her students might not understand everything that was happening in the play, from a metacognitive perspective she thought they could "think of the invisible workings of the mind when they write dialogue expressing certain thoughts or feelings" (p. 47). In justifying her decision and her belief in the use of drama, Lancer also echoes Heath (1993), saying, "In fact, drama has the potential to tap into such a wide range of linguistic abilities that it should be considered as a primary tool for teaching English as a second language" (p. 47). Lancer had read Worthman (2002), who believes that drama, as a social practice, is an authentic literacy experience; and Hanley and Gay (2002), who report that drama has been shown to improve writing, speaking, listening, and comprehension skills as students explore multiple interpretations and perspectives of a play.

Organizing, Supporting, and Scaffolding Learning

Lancer felt prepared for this project since she had attended two workshops on ways to teach Shakespeare. Originally she had planned a "speech by speech" analysis of Shakespeare's language, but then decided that technology was a better alternative. Using her collection of audiotapes and videotapes of different versions of the play could support her work and help her create enjoyable experiences for the students. She planned to use media and interactive Web sites to help her students make connections between the world of Shakespeare and modern day.

To start the project and to build students' background knowledge about life during the Italian Renaissance, Lancer arranged a class visit to the Medici collection at the Chicago Art Institute. Then, students discussed what they knew about Shakespeare and enjoyed creating Elizabethan insults.

Afterwards, Lancer explained the project to students: they would read *Romeo and Juliet*, watch several different versions of the play on video, and write their own version of the play. Lancer originally planned to read the play first and then allow students to write their own versions, but because of time constraints, she decided to have students read and write at the same time. Lancer also explained to students the reasons for watching multiple versions of the play with the understanding that the students' written play had to be original. Students could use computers to help with the writing process. Parents were informed of the nature of the activity and were asked for written permission for their children to watch different versions of *Romeo and Juliet*.

Before they started reading the play itself, Lancer and the whole class read the prologue chorally several times to learn about the importance of punctuation in understanding the text, and in order to get the correct intonation. Students learned new vocabulary words that they would encounter in the text.

During the second day, students were divided into five groups (three with girls and two with boys). Each team worked on their own play independently; at the end of the project the whole class would decide whether to combine parts or to select the best one for the class to perform. When students started writing, individual and group conferences with the teacher took place to support the use of required conventions.

Students read a scene from the original play; then they viewed videotapes of the same scene, and began their writing for the day. Some of the videotapes included ballet scenes, which the boys were not sure they liked, but eventually they found it relevant to their assignment. During the second week of the project, the class saw scenes from the film version of *West Side Story* (Robbins & Wise, 1961). At first, the boys were apprehensive about the amount of dancing in the film, but they found many familiar elements like gangs, Spanish language, blue jeans, and the urban setting. Eventually, they enjoyed the dancing, and the film enhanced their enthusiasm for writing their own version.

During group discussions about the writing, Lancer reported that one of the groups of girls decided to have their discussions in Spanish even though they were writing in English. Interactions between that group and the other groups were in Spanish, while all the other groups interacted in English. Lancer respected the group's use of their native language, as long as they were on-task.

As the activity developed, Lancer provided considerable sheltered instruction for her students. Students were also given written homework assignments in addition to their writing of the play. In one assignment, students pretended to be Juliet writing a letter to her father and telling him that she might marry Paris. To the teacher's surprise, both boys and girls were very responsive to these types of assignments.

Lessons Learned

Lancer (2005) made some important observations about the different responses of boys and girls to the project. All students were very serious and excited about the project. Early in the process, a boys' group complained that one of their members was writing only swear words, and they wanted him out of their group. Lancer had decided to accept whatever language the students produced, and cursing was certainly part of their community environment. As time went by, Lancer explained that "the novelty of being able to write swear words wore off when the hard work of writing a whole play became apparent to the groups" (p. 52). By the end of the project, that group member loved the play and started checking out books by Shakespeare from the library.

Another boy who was disengaged at first became the scribe for his team and, having found his niche, often typed his group's writing on the computer. Lancer reported that, in general, the boys reacted very positively to the "ownership aspect of the playwriting project" (p. 52). The boys concentrated on violence in their writing, which reflects the reality of their everyday life in the city.

The girls, however, enjoyed the social aspects of the activity. They were very good at creating romance in their stories, but they had trouble with tragedy and the elements that led to it.

Lancer felt that allowing children to use the knowledge and the language that they bring from their home and the community into a school activity made the children more motivated to learn, and it also helped them stay on-task. The nature of the project encouraged all students to increase their engagement in the practice of literacy. In the process, they were exposed to the arts and the use of technology. Lancer stated that her students "missed some of the meaning, but my class knows this play, the characters, and the themes. They will always know it. They own *Romeo and Juliet*" (p. 52).

Summary

These examples show how it is possible for teachers to learn about and develop ideas that tie the school curriculum to knowledge that exists in the students' homes and the community. This brings more cultural relevance into the curriculum and facilitates school learning. The two teachers described in this section were making school-to-home connections. They were making contributions, as the parents did in Part II of this book, to the creation of a bridge between home and school, in support of all children's learning and school success.

Epilogue
Reflections on the Road Traveled

In 1989, when I first started working in family literacy with Latinos in Chicago, I was aware of the important role that parents play in their children's early learning. Parents are the first and most important teachers for their young children. However, at that point, I did not recognize the value of the knowledge that exists in children's homes and communities, and I thought the role of a family literacy program was to show parents how to teach literacy to their children at home in mainstream ways. After all, researchers such as Epstein (1984a, 1987, 1995) have called for schools and teachers to stop talking about the lack of parental involvement in their school activities, and instead start teaching parents how they can get involved in their children's learning. Also, research by Goldenberg et al. (1992) has described how Latino parents supported their children's learning once the teacher told them how.

When we originally designed Project FLAME (Rodríguez-Brown & Shanahan, 1989), we never observed or tried to learn about the types of family literacy practiced by the families for which the program was designed. Today, I think that it was a major mistake on our part. Family literacy exists in all homes, regardless of income, education, or ethnicity. Parents and children engage in and are exposed to all kinds of literacy in their daily lives. Parents are also influenced by their own family's literacy and by the different ways in which they became literate. Parents then share their literacy knowledge in different ways with their children. In a diverse society, cultural ways of learning and differences in discourse make it almost impossible to think that there is a common way and similar types of knowledge that all parents share with their children. The role of family literacy programs then, even those created from a top-down perspective such as FLAME was initially, is to share knowledge about literacy teaching and learning with parents that allows families to add new activities to the ways in which they already share and practice literacy at home.

Reflecting on the success of Project FLAME, I think that if we had kept a top-down perspective, in which we taught parents what we thought they needed to know about helping their children at home, it would not have lasted for 19 years. We are grateful that within the first few years of the program, some of us discovered and recognized the value of the community and families' voices. It was then that we realized the need to consider parents' ideas and cultural ways of learning when planning activities. We began to make adaptations to the program activities, and we started offering services in ways that allow participants to take ownership of their learning. Some examples worth mentioning involve the changes to the ESL component and the creation of the Training of Trainers module of the program.

The ESL component was created to facilitate recruitment of families to the program and also to provide opportunities for children to see their parents as models of literacy learning. Originally, the ESL classes were designed for parents to learn grammar and vocabulary, to read simple texts, and do some structured writing. At first, parents were happy to attend those traditional classes. They thought that what they needed was a solid foundation in English grammar. However, they were not able to use what they were learning in class in their daily lives. Finally, we surveyed parents to ask what and how they wanted to learn English. After analyzing their responses, we decided that a participatory approach (Auerbach, 1989), based more on communicative competence and using topics of interest to the parents, was more relevant to the expressed needs of the parents. The participatory approach changed the structure of the lessons so that now parents learn the conversational English they need to do things like call the school or the doctor's office. Parents have found new functions for writing, beyond what they originally used. Today, FLAME participants are able to fill out forms and job applications if they need to do so. Although our main goal is NOT for them to find jobs, the program indirectly has supported those efforts. The participatory approach has been quite successful in attracting and keeping participants in the FLAME program.

An addition to the program that was designed as a result of listening to participants' needs and opinions is called the Training of Trainers. Through this module, we have been able to train parents to teach other parents from the school community where the programs are located how to conduct FLAME sessions. During this training, participants become partners with the FLAME teachers (university students) in the planning of activities for each literacy session. In the process, the content of the family literacy sessions is connected with existing knowledge and practices and becomes more relevant to the participants in each individual setting.

It was because of our success in adapting program activities to the needs of FLAME parents that we decided to develop a sociocultural framework and a set of principles to inform our everyday work with the participant families. We firmly believe that parents have a role in supporting their children's learning, and we believe that they should share literacy with their children in ways that are culturally relevant for their family. We respect the ways in which they share literacy with their children; we respect their knowledge and encourage them to share it with their children using their primary discourse and the language they know better.

Currently, the FLAME program provides parents with new information and practices to enrich their existing repertoire of literacy practices. In some ways, we are teaching parents about literacy practices that will support their children's transition to school, although we would prefer that they practice them at home in ways that are different from those the children use at school. For example, Latino parents might use storytelling rather than read alouds as a way to get their children interested in stories in books. Parents might also initiate an activity and then invite their children to participate with them.

For many people involved in family literacy programs, teaching parents how to support literacy learning at home is a way to create continuity between the home and the school. The more I work with parents who are culturally and linguistically different from the mainstream for which schools were created, the more I realize that teachers and schools also have to contribute to what I call the home–school connection. To me, as explained earlier, the home–school connection is a two-way street. Influenced by the work of Norma Gonzalez and Luis Moll with their Funds of Knowledge project (described in Chapter 7), and the work of teachers who believe in involving parents and bringing out-of-school knowledge into the school curriculum (as described in Chapters 8 and 9), I believe that it is important for teacher education programs to prepare prospective teachers by showing them ways to establish and maintain a home–school connection, regardless of the culture of their students. Understanding how to involve parents in their children's literacy education, while respecting their cultural ways of learning and discourse, and including parents' and community knowledge in school learning will create continuity between the home and school. This connection is particularly important for teachers who work in diverse settings because it can help to make the curriculum relevant for all children.

It is my hope that, through this book, readers become aware of the importance of parental involvement, and particularly family literacy (defined as learning at home), in increasing the continuity in learning between home and school and providing a relevant learning environment for all children.

Appendix
Sample Lesson from Project FLAME Manual

Project Flame Family Literacy Curriculum

Lesson 6: TEACHING THE ABCs

This lesson demonstrates simple ways to teach letters and sounds. The emphasis is on language, games, songs, and language experience activities.

Materials:
- *Copies of nursery rhymes, simple songs, and word games in native language or English.*
- *Construction paper or index cards, newspapers, magazines, and catalogs.*
- *Set of refrigerator magnets (optional).*

Write down any other materials you might need to find and bring for your particular lesson.

Objectives:
- *Parents will understand how to increase their children's phonemic awareness.*
- *Parents will effectively teach their children the letters of the alphabet.*
- *Parents will teach their children the sounds of the letters.*

Follow up:
Think of a question to ask parents about how they implemented ideas from the previous lesson and write it here:

_____

_____

I. Introductory Activity

One of the ways that teachers show children about words and letters is to play language games. Learning to listen for the differences between letter sounds like p/b, m/n, or t/d and practicing letter-sound associations are important skills for reading and writing. One of the best ways parents can help young children become aware of sounds is to teach them rhymes and songs.

In the past some of the introductory activities have included:

- Having students sing the ABC song while holding up the letter signs or marching to the vowel song holding up the letter signs.
- Giving students an example of a song, poem, or rhyme that uses repetition of the target sound, for example, "Jack and Jill" or "*Que llueva*." Then, have parents try to think of an example of their own to share with the class.
- Brainstorm a discussion question such as the one below and write the answers on the board or chart paper.

> **What are some of the different ways a child can learn the ABCs?**

Can you think of a different activity to introduce the idea of teaching the ABCs?

_____

_____

Explain to parents that the children who do best in school are those whose parents have taught them about letters and letter sounds (like Sesame Street does). This session will demonstrate more ways they can help their children with this important part of school learning.

II. Discussion

Here are some questions that introduce this topic in greater detail. You can choose from these questions or use your own. You should discuss four to six questions.

The group can discuss them as a class, in small groups, or with a partner. You can write them on note cards or on the board. Share your answers by recording their ideas and responses on the board or on chart paper:

1 *Have you taught your children the alphabet in Spanish or English? How did you do it?*
2 *Why is it important to teach children the letters and their sounds?*
3 *How can you teach the ABCs through everyday activities?*
4 *Why do you think it is important to teach children the ABCs in their native language?*
5 *When should a parent start to teach the ABCs?*
6 *How do you teach your children the sounds of letters?*
7 *How can you integrate teaching the ABCs into daily family life?*
8 *What resources do you know about that can help you with this work?*

Can you think of other questions to get parents talking about teaching the ABCs?

III. Alphabet Game Stations

Set up several different stations with different activities for teaching the ABCs. Have the parents spend a few minutes at each station to get an idea of how to do the activity at home with their children. Here are some ideas you can use at the different stations. Try to create your own game or activity too!

- *Alphabet Bingo*: Create four or five bingo cards with different arrangements of letters. Provide something for parents to cover the letters on the bingo cards. Write the letters on separate small sheets of paper and place them in an envelope. Place the B-I-N-G-O letters in another envelope. Randomly pick one letter from each envelope. Parents cover the letters as they are called. The first person to cover five letters across, diagonal, or horizontal wins.
- *Sorting*: Sort pictures or objects by beginning or ending letter sounds. Provide children with a quantity of items and ask them to sort the items by the letter or sound they begin with. For example, the child can pull out all the things that start with the letter "B."
- *Creating ABC flashcards*: Using index cards, have parents create

flashcards with the letter on one side and a picture that corresponds to the letter. Parents can draw or cut pictures from magazines.

- *Letter Mini-Books*: Make booklets of words and pictures that begin with a certain letter, such as "B." Write the letter on each page and the name of each item below its picture.

- *What's missing?* Write the alphabet, leaving some spaces for children to fill in. Write children's names or other words/names the children know, omitting some letters. Sing the alphabet song, pausing for children to insert the next letter.

- *"Go Fish"*: Write letters of the alphabet on index cards. You may want two sets for a larger group. Deal out five cards to each player. Parents take turns asking each other "Do you have an _____" for each letter. If the person asked has the card with the letter on it they must give it to the person asking. If not, they must "Go Fish" in the pile of cards in the center. Once they have a pair, they place them on the table. The goal is to get the most pairs of cards and to get rid of all your cards.

- *Memory*: Write letters of the alphabet on index cards. You can write another set of the alphabet on index cards or use pictures that correspond to the letters. Turn the cards over on the table. Parents take turns trying to make pairs.

- *Slap*: Write letters of the alphabet on index cards and place them on the table facing up. One person calls out a letter and the players must find the card and slap it. The person who slaps the card first gets to pick it up.

- *Name art*: Provide magazines, catalogs, and newspapers. Cut out the large letters that spell out your name from the magazine, and paste them on a piece of construction paper. Then decorate the rest of the page with other pictures if you wish.

- *Alphabet soup*: Provide parents with construction paper, glue, markers, and alphabet soup. Can the parents think of a creative activity with these materials?

 Remind parents that they can play alphabet games using the letter sounds or the actual letters.

IV. Wrapping It Up

Discuss teaching the ABCs with parents one last time. Depending on time, maybe choose just one question to discuss as a class.

1   How many letters should be taught at one time?
2   When should new letters be introduced? (When the first letter is known or the child asks about the letter.)
3   When could you play alphabet games with your children? How often? How long?
4   What should you do if your child gets bored or frustrated with a game or activity?

Think of another question and write it here:

_____

_____

_____

Your turn

V. Homework

•   Ask parents to make a book with their children based on one single letter sound. For example, they could make "My M Book." They can help a child make pictures of things that start with the letter "m." The child can label the pictures if they are able.

•   Have parents play one of the games with their children or make the "name art." Let parents know they will be discussing the success of the activity next time.

VI. Reflection

Reflect on your lesson. What did you most like? Why?

_____

_____

What happened that you didn't expect?

_____

_____

Your turn

What could you have done better?

_____

_____

Did you think of any other ideas you can use in the future?

_____

_____

References

Abi-Nader, J. (1991, April). *Family values and the motivation of Hispanic youth*. Paper presented at the annual meeting of the American Educational Research Association, Chicago, IL.

Abi-Nader, J. (1993). Meeting the needs of multicultural classrooms: Family values and the motivation of minority students. In M. J. O'Hair & S. J. Odell (Eds.), *Diversity and teaching* (pp. 212–228). Orlando, FL: Harcourt, Brace, & Jovanovich.

Ada, A. F. (1988). The Pajaro Valley experience: Working with Spanish-speaking parents to develop children's reading and writing skills in the home through the use of children's literature. In T. S. Skutnabb-Kangas & J. Cummins (Eds.), *Minority education: From shame to struggle* (pp. 223–238). Philadelphia, PA: Multilingual Matters.

Ada, A. F., & Zubizarreta, R. (2001). Parent narratives: The cultural bridge between Latino parents and their children. In *The best for our children: Critical perspectives on literacy for Latino students* (pp. 229–244). New York: Teachers College Press.

Amanti, C. (2005). Beyond a beads and feathers approach. In N. Gonzalez, L. Moll, & C. Amanti (Eds.), *Funds of knowledge: Theorizing practice in households, communities and classrooms* (pp. 131–142). Mahwah, NJ: Erlbaum.

American Association of School Administrators (AASA). (1998, Spring). Promoting parent involvement. *Leaders' Edge, 2*(2). Retrieved November 5, 2004, from www.aasa.org/publications/leaders_edge_Spring98.htm

Anderson, R., Wilson, P., & Fielding, L. (1988). Growth in reading and how children spend their time outside of school. *Reading Research Quarterly, 23*, 285–303.

Arroyo, L. (2003). *The home–school connection: Final research project*. Unpublished manuscript, University of Illinois at Chicago.

Auerbach, E. R. (1989). Toward a social-contextual approach to family literacy. *Harvard Educational Review, 59*, 165–181.

Auerbach, E. R. (1992). *Making meaning, making change: Participatory curriculum for adult ESL literacy*. McHenry, IL: Delta Systems.

Auerbach, E. R. (1995). Deconstructing the discourse of strengths in family literacy. *Journal of Reading Behavior, 27*, 643–661.

Baker, A. J. L. (1999). Opportunities at home and in the community that foster reading engagement. In J. T. Guthrie & D. E. Alvermann (Eds.), *Engaged reading: Processes, practices, and policy implications* (pp. 105–133). New York: Teachers College Press.

Baker, A. J. L., & Soden, L. M. (1997, April). *Parent involvement in children's education: A critical assessment of the knowledge base.* Paper presented at the annual meeting of the American Educational Research Association, Chicago, IL (ERIC Document Reproduction Service No. ED407127)

Baker, A. J. L., Piotrkowski, C. S., & Brooks-Gunn, J. (1998). The effects of the Home Instruction Program for Preschool Youngsters (HIPPY) on children's school performance at the end of the program and one year later. *Early Childhood Research Quarterly, 13,* 571–588.

Baker, A. J. L., Serpell, R., & Sonnenschein, S. (1995). Opportunities for learning in the homes of urban preschoolers. In L. M. Morrow (Ed.), *Family literacy: Connections in schools and communities* (pp. 236–252). Newark, DE: International Reading Association.

Baker, A. J. L., Sonnenschein, S., Serpell, R., Fernandez-Fein, S., & Scher, D. (1994). *Contexts of emergent literacy: Everyday home experiences of urban prekindergarten children* (Research Rep.). Athens, GA: National Reading Research Center, University of Georgia, and University of Maryland.

Banks, J. A. (1995). Multicultural education: Historical development, dimensions, and practice. In J. A. Banks & C. A. M. Banks (Eds.), *Handbook of research on multicultural education* (pp. 3–24). New York: Macmillan.

Beals, D., De Temple, J., & Dickinson, D. (1994). Talking and listening that support early literacy development of children from low-income families. In D. Dickinson (Ed.), *Bridges to literacy: Children, families and schools* (pp. 19–42). Cambridge, MA: Blackwell.

Bean, K. (2006). *Learning to book talk in fourth grade: Discourse change within a practice setting.* Unpublished doctoral dissertation, University of Illinois at Chicago.

Boehm, A. E. (1986). *Boehm test of basic concepts-revised.* San Antonio, TX: The Psychological Corporation/Harcourt, Brace, & Jovanovich.

Boethel, M. (2003). *Diversity: Schools, family and community connections. Annual Synthesis.* Austin, TX: National Center for Family and Community Connections with Schools.

Bowdoin Method. (n.d.). Retrieved June 27, 2005, from www.bowdoin-method.com/programs.html

Bright, J. A. (1996). Partners: An urban Black community perspective on the school and home working together. *New Schools, New Communities, 12*(3), 32–37.

Browning-Aiken, A. (2005). Border crossings: Funds of knowledge within an immigrant household. In N. Gonzalez, L. Moll, & C. Amanti (Eds.), *Funds of knowledge: Theorizing practice in households, communities and classroom* (pp. 167–182). Mahwah, NJ: Erlbaum.

Burguess, J. (1982). The effects of a training program for parents of preschoolers on the children's school readiness. *Reading Improvement, 19,* 313–318.

Cambourne, B. (2001). Conditions for literacy learning: Turning learning theory into classroom instruction: A minicase study. *The Reading Teacher, 54*, 414–418.

Carger, C. (1996). *Of borders and dreams*. New York: Teachers College Press.

Cazden, C. (1986). Classroom discourse. In M. C. Wittrock (Ed.), *Handbook of research on teaching* (3rd ed., pp. 432–463). New York: Macmillan.

Cazden, C. (1988). *Classroom discourse*. Portsmouth, NH: Heinemann.

Chandler J., Argyris, D., Barnes, W., Goodman, I., & Snow, C. (1985). Parents as teachers: Observations of low-income parents and children in a homework-like task. In B. Schieffelin & P. Gilmore (Eds.), *The acquisition of literacy: Ethnographic perspectives* (pp. 171–187). Norwood, NJ: Ablex.

Chavkin, N. F. (1989). Debunking the myth about minority parents. *Educational Horizons, 67*, 119–123.

Chavkin, N. F., & Gonzalez, D. L. (1995). *Forging partnerships between Mexican-American parents and the schools*. Morgantown, WV: ERIC Clearinghouse on Rural Education and Small Schools (ERIC Document Reproduction Service No. ED 388489)

Chavkin, N. F., & Williams, D. L., Jr. (1993). Minority parents and the elementary school: Attitudes and practices. In N. Chavkin (Ed.), *Families and schools in a pluralistic society* (pp. 673–683). Albany, NY: State University of New York Press.

Clay, M. M. (1979). *Stones—The concepts about print test*. Auckland, New Zealand: Heinemann.

Cochran, M. (1987). Empowering families: An alternative to the deficit model. In K. Hurrelmann, F. Kaufmann, & F. Losel (Eds.), *Social interventions: Potential and constraints* (pp. 105–120). New York: DeGruyter.

Cochran, M., & Dean, C. (1991). Home-school relations and the empowerment process. *Elementary School Journal, 91*, 261–269.

Cole, M., & Griffin, P. (1986). A socio-historical approach to remediation. In S. deCastell, K. Egan, & A. Luke (Eds.), *Literacy, society and schooling: A reader* (pp. 110–131). London: Cambridge University Press.

Cotton, K., & Wakelund, K. R. (1989). *Parent involvement in education* (SIRS Close-up #6). Portland, OR: Northwest Regional Educational Laboratory. Retrieved August 22, 2004, from www.nwrel.org/scpd/sirs/3cu6.html

Crowe, C. (2004). Wonderful Wednesdays. *Responsive Classroom Newsletter, 16*(4), 1–4.

Cushman, E. (1998). *The struggle and the tools: Oral literacy strategies in an inner-city community*. New York: SUNY Press.

D'Andrade, R. (1995). *The development of cognitive anthropology*. Cambridge, England: Cambridge University Press.

Darling, S. (1997, March). *Opening session speech*. Paper presented at the Sixth Annual Conference on Family Literacy, Louisville, KY.

Dauber, S. L., & Epstein, J. L. (1989). Parents' attitudes and practices of involvement in inner-city elementary and middle schools. In N. Chavkin (Ed.), *Families and schools in a pluralistic society* (pp. 53–71). Albany, NY: State University of New York Press.

De Avila, E. A., & Duncan, S. E. (1987). *The language assessment scales (LAS)*. Monterrey, CA: CTB/McGraw-Hill.

De Avila, E. A., & Duncan, S. E. (1993). *The adult-language assessment scales (A-LAS)*. Monterrey, CA: CTB/McGraw-Hill.

De Bruin-Parecki, A., Paris, S. G., & Seidenberg, J. L. (1996). *Characteristics of effective family literacy programs in Michigan*. (NCAL Technical Report TR96–07). Ann Arbor, MI: University of Michigan, National Center on Adult Literacy.

Delgado-Gaitan, C. (1987). Mexican adult literacy: New directions for immigrants. In S. R. Goldman & H. Trueba (Eds.), *Becoming literate in English as a second language* (pp. 9–32). Norwood, NJ: Ablex.

Delgado-Gaitan, C. (1992). School matters in the Mexican-American home: Socializing children to education. *American Educational Research Journal, 29*, 495–513.

Delgado-Gaitan, C. (1993). Research and policy in reconceptualizing family-schools relationships. In P. Phelan & A. Locke-Davidson (Eds.), *Renegotiating cultural diversity in American schools* (pp. 139–158). New York: Teachers College Press.

Delgado-Gaitan, C. (2001). *The power of community: Mobilizing for family and schooling*. Lanham, MD: Rowman and Littlefield.

Delpit, L. (1995). *Other people's children: Cultural conflict in the classroom*. New York: New Press.

Desimone, L. (1999). Linking parent involvement with student achievement: Do race and income matter? *The Journal of Educational Research, 93*(1), 11–30.

Doake, D. (1985). Reading-like behavior: Its role in learning to read. In A. Jagger & M. T. Smith (Eds.), *Observing the language learner* (pp. 82–98). Newark, DE: International Reading Association.

Duncan, S. E., & De Avila, E. A. (1986). *Pre-language assessment scales (LAS)*. Monterrey, CA: CTB/McGraw-Hill.

Dyson, A. H. (2003). *The brothers and sisters learn to write: Popular literacies in childhood and school cultures*. New York: Teachers College Press.

Edwards, P. A. (1988, December). *Lower SES mothers' learning of book reading strategies*. Paper presented at the annual meeting of the National Reading Conference, Tucson, AZ.

Edwards, P. A. (1995). Empowering low-income mothers and fathers to share books with young children. *The Reading Teacher, 48*, 558–564.

Epstein, J. L. (1984a). School policy and parent involvement: Research results. *Educational Horizons, 62*, 70–72.

Epstein, J. L. (1984b, April). *Effects of teacher practices of parent involvement for change of students' achievement in reading and math*. Paper presented at the annual meeting of the American Educational Research Association, New Orleans, LA.

Epstein, J. L. (1986). Parents' reactions to teacher practices of parent involvement. *Elementary School Journal, 86*, 277–294.

Epstein, J. L. (1987). Toward a theory of family-school connections: Teacher practices and parent involvement. In F. Hurrelman, F. Kauffman, & F. Losel (Eds.), *Social intervention: Potential and constraints* (pp. 121–136). New York: DeGruyter.

Epstein, J. L. (1991). Effects on student achievement of teachers' practices of parent involvement. In S. Silvern (Ed.), *Literacy through family, community, and school interaction* (pp. 261–276). Greenwich, CT: JAI Press.

Epstein, J. L. (1992). *School and family partnerships* (Report No. 6). Baltimore, MD: Center for Families and Communities, Schools and Children's Learning, Johns Hopkins University.

Epstein, J. L. (1995). School-family-community partnerships: Caring for the children we share. *Phi Delta Kappan, 76*, 701–712.

Epstein, J. L. (Ed.). (2001). *School, family and community partnerships: Preparing educators and improving schools.* Boulder, CO: Westview Press.

Erickson, F. (1993). Transformation and school success: The politics and culture of educational achievement. In E. Jacob & C. Jordan (Eds.), *Minority education: Anthropological perspectives* (pp. 27–52). Westport, CT: Greenwood.

Espinosa, L. M. (1995). *Hispanic parent involvement in early childhood programs.* ERIC Clearinghouse on Elementary and Early Childhood Education (ERIC Document Reproduction Service No. ED382412)

Fairclough, N. (1992). *Discourses and social change.* Cambridge, England: Polity Press.

Feiltelson, D., & Goldstein, Z. (1986). Patterns of book ownership and reading to young children in Israeli school-oriented and non-school-oriented families. *Reading Teacher, 39*, 924–930.

Fields, J., & Casper, L. M. (2001). *America's families and living arrangement: March 2000.* (Current Population Reports, P20–537). Washington, DC: U.S. Census Bureau.

Flaxman, E., & Inger, M. (1992). Parents and schooling in the 1990s. *Principal, 72*(7), 16–18.

Flores, B., Cousin, P. T., & Diaz, E. (1991). Transforming the deficit myths about learning, language and culture. *Language Arts, 68*, 369–379.

Foster, M. (1995). African American teachers and culturally relevant pedagogy. In J. A. Banks & C. A. M. Banks (Eds.), *Handbook of research in multicultural education* (pp. 570–581). New York: Macmillan.

Gallimore, R., & Goldenberg, C. N. (1989, April). *Social effects on emergent literacy experiences in families of Spanish-speaking children.* Paper presented at the annual meeting of the American Educational Research Association, San Francisco, CA.

Gallimore, R., & Reese, L. J. (1999). Mexican immigrants in urban California: Forging adaptations from familiar and new cultural resources. In M. C. Foblets & C. I. Pang (Eds.), *Culture, ethnicity and immigration* (pp. 245–263). Leuven, Belgium: ACCO.

Gallimore, R., Boggs, J. W., & Jordan, C. (1974). *Culture, behavior and education: A study of Hawaiian-Americans.* Beverly Hills, CA: Sage.

Gee, J. P. (1989). What is literacy? *Journal of Education, 171*, 18–25.

Gee, J. P. (1996). *Social linguistics and literacies: Ideologies in discourses.* London: Farmer Press.

Gee, J. P. (1999). *An introduction to discourse analysis: Theory and method.* New York: Routledge.

Gibson, M. A. (2002). The new Latino diaspora and educational policy. In

S. Wortham, E. G. Murillo, & E. T. Hamann (Eds.), *Education in the new Latino diaspora: Policy and the politics of identity* (pp. 241–252). Westport, CT: Ablex.

Gladsden, V. L. (1994). Understanding family literacy: Conceptual issues facing the field. *Teachers College Record, 96*, 58–86.

Gladsden, V. L. (1996). Designing and conducting family literacy programs that account for racial, ethnic, religious, and other cultural differences. In L. A. Benjamin & J. Lord (Eds.), *Family literacy: Directions in research and implications for practice* (pp. 31–38). Washington, DC: U.S. Department of Education.

Goldenberg, C. N. (1987). Low-income Hispanic parents' contributions to their first-grade children's word recognition skills. *Anthropology of Education Quarterly, 18*, 149–179.

Goldenberg, C. N. (1989). Parents' effects on academic grouping for reading: Three case studies. *American Educational Research Journal, 26*, 329–352.

Goldenberg, C. N., & Gallimore, R. (1991). Local knowledge, research knowledge, and educational change: A case study of early reading improvement. *Educational Researcher, 20*, 2–14.

Goldenberg, C. N., & Gallimore, R. (1995). Immigrant Latino parents' values and beliefs about their children's education: Continuities and discontinuities across cultures and generations. In P. Pintrich & M. Maehr (Eds.), *Advances in motivation and achievement* (Vol. 9, pp. 183–228). Greenwich, CN: Ablex.

Goldenberg, C. N., Reese, L., & Gallimore, R. (1992). Effects of literacy materials from school on Latino children's home experiences and early reading achievement. *American Journal of Education, 100*, 497–536.

Gonzalez, N., Moll, L., & Amanti, C. (2005). Introduction: Theorizing practices. In N. Gonzalez, L. Moll, & C. Amanti (Eds.), *Funds of knowledge: Theorizing practice in households, communities and classrooms* (pp. 1–28). Mahwah, NJ: Erlbaum.

Gonzalez, N., Moll, L. D., Floyd-Tennery, M., Rivera, A., Rendon, P., & Amanti, C. (1993). Funds of knowledge for teaching in Latino households. *Urban Education, 29*(4), 443–470.

Good, R. H., & Kaminsky, R. A. (Eds.). (2002). *Dynamic indicators of basic early literacy skills* (6th ed.). Eugene, OR: Institute for the Development of Educational Achievement. Retrieved August 6, 2004, from http://dibels.uoregon.edu

Goodman, Y. (1986). Coming to know literacy. In W. Teale & E. Sulzby (Eds.), *Emergent literacy: Writing and reading* (pp. 1–14). Norwood, NJ: Ablex.

Gutiérrez, K. D., & Rogoff, B. (2003). Cultural ways of learning: Individual traits or repertoires of practice. *Educational Researcher, 32*(5), 15–25.

Gutiérrez, K. D., Baquedano-López, P., & Tejeda, C. (1999). Rethinking diversity: Hybridity and hybrid language practices in the third space. *Mind, Culture, & Activity: An International Journal, 6*, 286–303.

Gutiérrez, K. D., Baquedano-López, P., Alvarez, H., & Chiu, M. M. (1999). Building a culture of collaboration through hybrid language practices. *Theory Into Practice, 38*(2), 87–93.

Guzman, B. (2001). *The Hispanic population: Census 2000 Brief.* Washington, DC: U.S. Census Bureau. Retrieved August 8, 2006, from www.census. gov/prod/2004/pubs//censr_18.pdf

Hanley, M. S., & Gay, G. (2002). Teaching moral education and social action through drama. *Talking Points, 14*, 22–26.

Heath, S. B. (1983). *Ways with words: Language, life and work in community and classrooms.* Cambridge, England: Cambridge University Press.

Heath, S. B. (1986). Sociocultural context of language development. In California State Department of Education (Ed.), *Beyond language: Social and cultural factors in schooling language minority students* (pp. 143–186). Los Angeles, CA: Evaluation Dissemination and Assessment Center, California State University.

Heath, S. B. (1993). Inner city life through drama: Imagining the language classroom. *TESOL Quarterly, 27*, 177–192.

Heath, S. B., & McLaughlin, M. (Eds.). (1993). *Identity and inner city youth: Beyond ethnicity and gender.* New York: Teachers College Press.

Henderson, A. (1987). *The evidence continues to grow: Parent involvement improves achievement.* Columbia, MD: National Committee for Citizens in Education.

Henderson, A., & Berla, N. (Eds.). (1994). *A new generation of evidence: The family is critical to student achievement.* Washington, DC: National Committee for Citizens in Education, Center for Law and Education.

Henderson, A. T., & Mapp, K. L. (2002). *A new wave of evidence: The impact of school, family, and community connections on student achievement.* Retrieved August 6, 2004, from www.sedl.org/connections/resources. html

Hensley, M. (2005). Empowering parents of multicultural backgrounds. In N. Gonzalez, L. Moll, & C. Amanti (Eds.), *Funds of knowledge: Theorizing practice in households, communities and classrooms* (pp. 143–152). Mahwah, NJ: Erlbaum.

Hester, H. (1989). Start at home to improve home–school relations. *National Association of Secondary School Principals Bulletin, 73*(513), 23–27.

Hidalgo, N., Bright, J., Siu, S. F., Swap, S., & Epstein, J. L. (1995). Research on families, schools and communities: A multicultural perspective. In J. A. Banks & C. A. M. Banks (Eds.), *Handbook of research on multicultural education* (pp. 498–524). New York: Macmillan.

Hislop, N. (2000). *Hispanic parental involvement in home literacy.* ERIC Clearinghouse on Reading, English, and Communication (Eric Document Reproduction Service No. ED 446340)

Hull, G., & Schultz, K. (2002). *School's out! Bridging out-of-school literacy with classroom practice.* New York: Teachers College Press.

Illinois State Board of Education. (2004). *Illinois snapshot of early literacy.* Springfield, IL: Author. Retrieved August 6, 2006, from www. isbe.net/ils/ela/reading/html/isel.htm

Inger, M. (1992). *Increasing the school involvement of Hispanic parents.* ERIC Clearinghouse on Urban Education (ERIC Document Reproduction Service No. EDO-UD-92-3)

Jesse, D. (1998). *Increasing parent involvement: A key to student achievement.*

Retrieved September 27, 2004, from www.mcrel.org/topics/noteworthy-pages/noteworthy/danj.asp

Jeynes, W. H. (2003). A meta-analysis: The effects of parental involvement on minority children's academic achievement. *Education and Urban Society, 35*(2), 202–218.

Jones, R. (2001, September). How parents can support learning. *American School Board Journal, 188*(9). Retrieved August 26, 2004, from http://.asbj.com/2001/09/0901coverstory.html

Keith, P. B., & Lichtman, M. V. (1994). Does parental involvement influence the achievement of Mexican-American eighth graders? Results of the national longitudinal study. *School Psychology Quarterly, 89*(4), 256–272.

Knobel, M. (1999). *Everyday literacies: Students discourse and social practice.* New York: Peter Lang.

Kohl, G. O., Lengua, L. J., & McMahon, R. J. (2000). Parent involvement: Conceptualizing multiple dimensions and their relation with family and demographic risk factors. *Journal of School Psychology, 38*, 501–523.

Kyle, D., & McIntyre. E. (2000). *Family visits benefit teachers and families— and students most of all* (Practitioner Brief #1). Santa Cruz, CA: Center for Research on Education, Diversity, & Excellence, University of California. Retrieved March 23, 2006, from www.cal.org/crede/pubs/PracBrief1.htm

Kyle, D., McIntyre, E., Miller, K., & Moore, G. (2002). *Reaching-out: A K-5 resource for connecting families and schools.* Thousand Oaks, CA: Corwin Press.

Lancer, A. (2005). Using drama to access out-of-school literacy. *Illinois Reading Council Journal, 32*(2), 46–53.

Larsen, L. J. (2004). *The foreign-born population in the United States: 2003.* (Current Population Reports, P20–551). Washington, DC: U.S. Census Bureau.

Laureau, A. (1989). *Home advantage: Social class and parental intervention.* New York: Farmer Press.

Leitch, M. L., & Tangri, S. S. (1988). Barriers to home–school collaboration. *Educational Horizons, 66*, 70–74.

LeVine, R. (1977). Child rearing as cultural adaptation. In P. Leiderman, S. Tulkin, & A. Rosenfeld (Eds.), *Culture and infancy* (pp. 15–27). New York: Academic Press.

Lindle, J. C. (1989). What do parents want from principals and teachers? *Educational Leadership, 47*(2), 12–14.

Liontos, L. B. (1992). *At-risk families and schools becoming partners.* Eugene, OR: ERIC Clearinghouse on Educational Management.

Lopez, G. R. (2001). The value of hard work: Lessons on parent involvement from an (im)migrant household. *Harvard Education Review, 71*, 416–437.

McCarthey, S. J. (1997). Connecting home and school literacy practices in classrooms with diverse populations. *Journal of Literacy Research, 29*(2), 145–182

McCarthey, S. J. (1999). Identifying teacher practices that connect home and school. *Education and Urban Society, 32*(1), 83–107.

McCoy, L., & Watts, T. (1992). *Learning together: Family literacy in Ontario.* Kingston, Ontario, Canada: Family Literacy Interest Group of the Ontario Reading Association.

Mattingly, D. J., Prislin, R., McKenzie, T. L., Rodríguez, J. L., & Kayzar, B. (2002). Evaluating evaluations: The case of parent involvement programs. *Review of Educational Research, 72,* 549–576.

Medina, J. (2003). *The teacher for a day project.* Unpublished manuscript, University of Illinois at Chicago.

Mercado, C. I., & Moll, L. C. (1997). The study of funds of knowledge: Collaborative research in Latino homes. *CENTRO, The Journal of the Center for Puerto Rican Studies, IX(9),* 26–42.

MetriTech. (1987). *The Illinois reading assessment project: Literacy survey.* Champaign, IL: MetriTech.

Moles, O. (1994). Who wants parent involvement? *Education and Urban Society, 19,* 137–145.

Moll, L. C. (1992). Bilingual classroom studies and community analysis: Some recent trends. *Educational Researcher, 21(3),* 20–24.

Moll, L. C. (1994). Literacy research in community and classrooms: A sociocultural approach. In R. B. Ruddell, M. R. Ruddell, & H. Singer (Eds.), *Theoretical models and processes of reading* (pp. 179–207). Newark, DE: International Reading Association.

Moll, L. C. (1998). Turning to the world: Bilingual schooling, literacy, and the cultural mediation of thinking. *National Reading Conference Yearbook, 47,* 59–75.

Moll, L. C. (2005). Reflections and possibilities. In N. Gonzalez, L. Moll, & C. Amanti (Eds.), *Funds of knowledge: Theorizing practice in households, communities and classrooms* (pp. 275–288). Mahwah, NJ: Erlbaum.

Moll, L. C., & Greenberg, J. B. (1990). Creating zones of possibilities: Combining social contexts for instruction. In L. C. Moll (Ed.), *Vygotsky and education* (pp. 319–348). New York: Cambridge University Press.

Moll, L. C., Amanti, C., Neff, D., & Gonzalez, N. (1992). Funds of knowledge for teaching: Using a qualitative approach to connect homes and classrooms. *Theory Into Practice, 31,* 132–141.

Moneyhun, C. A. (1997, March). *"Work to be done": Community literacy as a new model of social action for literacy educators.* Paper presented at the annual meeting of the Conference on College Composition and Communication. Phoenix, AZ. (ERIC Document Reproduction Service No. 407–677)

Moore, E. K. (1991). Improving schools through parental involvement. *Principal, 71(1),* 17–20.

Morrow, L. M. (Ed.). (1995). *Family literacy: Connections in schools and communities.* Newark, DE: International Reading Association.

Mulhern, M. M. (1991). *The impact of a family literacy project on three Mexican-immigrant families.* Unpublished manuscript, University of Illinois at Chicago.

National Association of Elementary School Principals. (n.d.) Alexandria, VA. Retrieved August 26, 2004, from www.naesp.org

National Center for Family Literacy (NCFL). (1995). *Family literacy: An overview.* Louisville, KY: Author.

National Parent Teacher Association (2003). *Parent involvement policies and Title I. What parents need to know.* Retrieved August 26, 2004, from www.pta.org/parentinvolvement/helpchild/hc_piandlaw.asp

Networks of Educators on the Americas: Tellin'Stories. (n.d.). Retrieved August 26, 2004, from www.teachingforchange.org/DC_Projects/Telling_Stories/telling_stories.html

Nickse, R. (1989). *The noises of literacy: An overview of intergenerational and family literacy programs* (Report No. CE053–282). Boston, MA: Boston University (ERIC Document Reproduction Service No. ED 308415)

Nickse, R., Speicher, A. M., & Buchek, P. C. (1988). An intergenerational adult literacy project: A family intervention/prevention model. *Journal of Reading, 31*, 634–642.

Nieto, S. (1996). *Affirming diversity: The sociopolitical context of multicultural education* (2nd ed.). White Plains, NY: Longman.

Nieto, S. (2002). *Language, culture and teaching: Critical perspectives for a new century.* Mahwah, NJ: Erlbaum.

North Central Regional Education Laboratory (NCREL). (2004). Relationship between school climate and family involvement. In *Pathways to School Improvement.* Retrieved August 25, 2004 from: www.ncrel.org/sdrs/areas/issues/envrnmnt/famncomm/pa3lk5a.htm

Olmstead, P. P., & Rubin, R. I. (1983). Linking parent behaviors to child achievement: Four evaluation studies from the parent education Follow Through Program. *Studies in Educational Evaluation, 8*, 317–325.

Pappas, C., & Brown, E. (1988). The development of children's sense of the written story register: Analysis of the texture of kindergarteners' "pretend reading" texts. *Linguistics and Education, 1*, 45–79.

Paratore, J. R. (1993). Influence of an intergenerational approach to literacy on the practice of literacy of parents and their children. In C. Kinzer & D. Leu (Eds.), *Examining central issues in literacy research, theory and practice: 42nd Yearbook of the National Reading Conference* (pp. 83–91). Chicago, IL: National Reading Conference.

Paratore, J. R. (1994). Parents and children sharing literacy. In D. Lancy (Ed.), *Emergent literacy: From research to practice* (pp. 193–216). New York: Praeger.

Paratore, J. R. (2001). *Opening doors, opening opportunities. Family literacy in an urban community.* Needham Heights, MA: Allyn & Bacon.

Paratore, J. R., & Harrison, C. (1995). A themed issue on family literacy. *Journal of Reading, 38*, 516–517.

Paratore, J. R., Melzi, G., & Krol-Sinclair, B. (1999). *What should we expect from family literacy?: Experiences of Latino children whose parents participate in an intergenerational literacy project.* Newark, DE: IRA/NRC.

Parents as Teachers National Center, Inc. (n.d.). Retrieved November 5, 2004, from www.patnc.org

Peck, W. C., Flowers, L., & Higgins, L. (1995). Community Literacy. *College Composition and Communication, 46*, 199–222.

Powell, D. R. (1995, September). *Teaching parenting and basic skills to parents: What we know.* Paper presented at a Research Design Symposium on

Family Literacy. U.S. Department of Education, Office of Educational Research and Improvement, Washington, DC.

Public Agenda. (1999). *Playing their parts: What parents and teachers really mean by parent involvement.* Retrieved November 5, 2004, from www.publicagenda.orgspecials/parent/parent.htm

Purcell-Gates, V. (1988). Lexical and syntactic knowledge of written narrative held by well-read-to kindergartners and second graders. *Research in the Teaching of English, 22,* 128–160.

Purcell-Gates, V. (1995). *Other people's words: The cycle of illiteracy.* Cambridge, MA: Harvard University Press.

Purcell-Gates, V. (1996). Stories, coupons, and the TV Guide: Relationships between home literacy experiences and emergent literacy knowledge. *Reading Research Quarterly, 31,* 406–428.

Quezada, S., & Nickse, R. S. (1993). *Community collaborations for family literacy handbook.* New York: Neal-Shuman.

Quintero, E., & Huerta-Macias, A. (1990a). All in the family: Bilingualism and biliteracy. *The Reading Teacher, 44,* 306–312.

Quintero, E., & Huerta-Macias, A. (1990b). Learning together: Issues for language minority parents and their children. *Journal of Educational Issues of Language Minority Students, 10,* 41–56.

Ramirez, R., & de la Cruz, P. (2003). *The Hispanic population in the United States: March 2002* (Current Population Reports, P20–545). Washington, DC: U.S. Census Bureau.

Reese, L., & Gallimore, R. (2000). Immigrant Latinos' cultural models of literacy development: An alternative perspective on home–school discontinuities. *American Journal of Education, 108,* 103–134.

Reese, L., Balzano, S., Gallimore, R., & Goldenberg, C. (1995). The concept of "educación": Latino family values and American schooling. *International Journal of Educational Research, 23*(1), 57–81.

Reese, L., Gallimore, R., & Goldenberg, C. N. (1999). Job-required literacy, home literacy environments, and school reading: Early literacy experiences of immigrant Latino children. In J. G. Lipson & L. A. McSpadden (Eds.), *Negotiating power and place at the margins: Selected papers on refugees and immigrants* (Vol. VII, pp. 232–269). Washington, DC: American Anthropological Association.

Reese, L., Garnier, H., Gallimore, R., & Goldenberg, C. (2000). Longitudinal analysis of the antecedents of emergent Spanish literacy and middle school reading achievement of Spanish-speaking students. *American Educational Research Journal, 6,* 633–662.

Reynolds, A. J., Temple, J. A., Robertson, D. L., & Mann, E. A. (2001). Long-term effects of an early childhood intervention on educational achievement and juvenile arrest: A 15-year follow-up of low-income children in public schools. *Journal of the American Medical Association, 285,* 2339–2446.

Rich, D. (1985). *The forgotten factor in school success: The family.* Washington, DC: Home and School Institute.

Rich, D. (1993). Building the bridge to reach minority parents: Education infrastructure supporting success for all children. In N. Chavkin (Ed.), *Famil-*

ies and schools in a pluralistic society (pp. 235–244). Albany, NY: State University of New York Press.

Ritter, P. L., Mount-Reynaud, R., & Dornbusch, S. M. (1992). Minority parents and their youth: Concern, encouragement, and support for school achievement. In N. Chavkin (Ed.), *Families and schools in a pluralistic society* (pp. 107–119). Albany, NY: State University of New York Press.

Robbins, J., & Wise, R. (Directors). (1961). *West side story* [Motion picture]. United States: MGM/UA Studios.

Rodríguez-Brown, F. V. (2001a). Home-school collaboration: Successful models in the Hispanic community. In P. Mosenthal & P. Schmitt (Eds.), *Reconceptualizing literacy in the new age of pluralism and multiculturalism, Advances in reading and language research* (pp. 273–288). Greenwich, CT: Information Age Publishing.

Rodríguez-Brown, F. V. (2001b). Home-school connections in a community where English is the second language. In V. Risko & K. Bromley (Eds.), *Collaboration for diverse learners: Viewpoints and practices* (pp. 273–288). Newark, DE: International Reading Association.

Rodríguez-Brown, F. V. (2003). Reflections on family literacy from a sociocultural perspective. *Reading Research Quarterly, 38*, 146–153.

Rodríguez-Brown, F. V. (2004). Project FLAME: A parent support family literacy model. In B. Wasik (Ed.), *Handbook of family literacy* (pp. 213–229). Mahwah, NJ: Erlbaum.

Rodríguez-Brown, F. V., & Meehan, M. A. (1998). Family literacy and adult education: Project FLAME. In C. Smith (Ed.), *Literacy for the twentieth-first century* (pp. 176–193). Westport, CT: Praeger.

Rodríguez-Brown, F. V., & Mulhern, M. M. (1993). Fostering critical literacy through family literacy: A study of families in a Mexican-immigrant community. *Bilingual Research Journal, 17*(3/4), 1–16.

Rodríguez-Brown, F. V., & Shanahan, T. (1989). *Literacy for the limited English proficient child: A family approach.* [Proposal submitted to OBEMLA/USDE, under the Title VII ESEA Family Literacy Program.] Unpublished manuscript, University of Illinois at Chicago.

Rodríguez-Brown, F. V., Li, R. F., & Albom, J. A. (1999). Hispanic parents' awareness and use of literacy-rich environments at home and in the community. *Education and Urban Society, 32*, 41–57.

Rogers, R. (2001). Family literacy and cultural models. *National Reading Conference Yearbook, 50*, 96–114.

Rogers, R. (2002). Between contexts: A critical analysis of family literacy, discursive practices and literacy subjectivities. *Reading Research Quarterly, 37*, 248–277.

Rogers, R. (2003). *A critical discourse analysis of family literacy practices: Power in and out of print.* Mahwah, NJ: Erlbaum.

Rogoff, B. (1990). *Apprenticeship in thinking: Cognitive development in social context.* New York: Oxford University Press.

Rogoff, B., Gauvain, M., & Ellis, S. (1984). Development viewed in its cultural context. In M. H. Bornstein & M. E. Lamb (Eds.), *Developmental psychology: An advanced text* (pp. 533–571). Hillsdale, NJ: Erlbaum.

Sable, J., & Stennett, J. (1998). The educational progress of Hispanic students.

In *The condition of education 1998* (pp. 11–19). (NCES Report). Washington, DC: U.S. Department of Education.

Scott-Jones, D. (1993). Parents and educators in a pluralistic society. In N. F. Chavkin (Ed.), *Families and schools in a pluralistic society* (pp. 245–254). Albany, NY: State University of New York Press.

Scribner, J. D., Young, M. D., & Pedroza, A. (1999). Building collaborative relationships with parents. In P. Reyes, J. D. Scribner, & A. P. Scribner (Eds.), *Lessons from high-performing Hispanic schools: Creating learning communities* (pp. 36–60). New York: Teachers College Press.

Shanahan, T., Mulhern, M., & Rodríguez-Brown, F. V. (1995). Project FLAME: Lessons learned from a family literacy program for linguistic minority families. *The Reading Teacher, 48,* 586–593.

Silvern, S. (1988). Continuity/discontinuity between home and early childhood education environments. *Elementary School Journal, 89,* 147–160.

Skilton-Sylvester, E. (2002). Literate at home but not at school: A Cambodian girl's journey from playwright to struggling writer. In G. Hull & K. Schultz (Eds.), *School's out!: Bridging out-of-school literacies with classroom practice* (pp. 61–90). New York: Teachers College Press.

Snow, C., & Tabors, P. (1996). Intergenerational transfer of literacy. In L. A. Benjamin & J. Lord. (Eds.), *Family literacy: Directions in research and implications for practice* (pp. 73–80). Washington, DC: U.S. Department of Education, Office of Educational Research and Improvement.

Taylor, D. (1983). *Family literacy: Young children learning to read and write.* Exeter, NH: Heinemann.

Taylor, D., & Dorsey-Gaines, C. (1988). *Growing up literate: Learning from inner-city families.* Portsmouth, NH: Heinemann.

Teale, W. H. (1984). Reading to young children: Its significance for literacy development. In H. Goelman, A. Oberg, & F. Smith (Eds.), *Awakening to literacy* (pp. 110–121). Portsmouth, NH: Heinemann.

Teale, W. H. (1986). Home background and young children's literacy development. In W. H. Teale & E. Sulsby (Eds.), *Emergent literacy: Writing and reading* (pp. 173–206). Norwood, NJ: Ablex.

Teale, W. H., & Sulzby, E. (Eds.). (1986). *Emergent literacy: Writing and reading.* Norwood, NJ: Ablex.

Tenery, M. F. (2005). La Visita. In N. Gonzalez, L. Moll, & C. Amanti (Eds.), *Funds of knowledge: Theorizing practice in households, communities and classrooms* (pp. 119–130). Mahwah, NJ: Erlbaum.

Tharp, R. G. (1989). Culturally compatible education: A formula for designing effective classrooms. In H. T. Trueba, G. Spindler, & L. Spindler (Eds.), *What do anthropologists have to say about dropouts?* (pp. 51–66). New York: Farmer Press.

The New London Group. (1996). A pedagogy of multiliteracies: Designing social futures. *Harvard Educational Review, 66*(1), 60–62.

The Parent Institute. Fairfax, VA. (n.d.). *What is working on parent involvement.* Retrieved August 26, 2004, from www.parentinstitute.com

Tobin, A. W. (1981). *A multiple discriminant cross validation of the factors associated with the development of precocious reading development.* Unpublished doctoral dissertation, University of Delaware.

Trueba, H., Jacobs, L., & Kirton, E. (1990). *Cultural conflict and adaptation: The case of Hmong children in American society.* New York: Farmer Press.

Trumbull, E., Rothstein-Fish, C., Greenfield, P. M., & Quiroz, B. (2001). *Bridging cultures between home and schools: A guide for teachers.* Mahwah, NJ: Erlbaum.

United States. (2000). *Literacy Involves Families Together Act (Report together with additional and dissenting views (to accompany H.R. 3222) including cost estimate of the Congressional Budget Office).* Washington, DC: U.S. Government Publications Office.

United States. (2001). *No Child Left Behind Act of 2001.* Washington, DC: U.S. Government Publications Office.

Valdes, G. (1996). *Con respeto: Bridging the differences between culturally diverse families and schools.* New York: Teachers College Press.

Vandergrift, J. A., & Greene, A. L. (1992). Rethinking parent involvement. *Educational Leadership, 50*(1), 57–59.

Van Fossen, S., & Sticht, T. G. (1991). *Teach the mother and reach the child: Results of the intergenerational literacy action research project.* Washington, DC: Wider Opportunities for Women.

Vélez-Ibañez, C., & Greenberg, J. (1992). Formation and transformation of funds of knowledge. *Anthropology and Education Quarterly, 23,* 313–335.

Wagner, M., & Spiker, D. (2001). *Multisite parents as teachers' evaluation: Experience and outcomes for children and families.* Menlo Park, CA: SRI International. Retrieved June 27, 2005, from www.parentsasteachers.org/site/pp.asp?c = ekIRLcMZJxE&b = 307807

Walberg, H. J. (1984). Improving the productivity of American schools. *Educational Leadership, 41,* 19–27.

Weisner, T. (1997). The ecocultural project of human development: Why ethnography and its findings matter. *Ethos, 25,* 1977–1990.

Weisner, T., Gallimore, R., & Jordan, C. (1988). Unpackaging cultural effects on classroom learning: Native Hawaiian peer assistance and child-generated activity. *Anthropology and Education Quarterly, 19,* 327–353.

Weisz, E. (1990). Developing positive staff-parent partnerships in high schools. *American Secondary Education, 19*(1), 25–28.

Wells, G. (1986). *The meaning makers.* Portsmouth, NH: Heinemann.

Wheeler, M. E. (1971). *Untutored acquisition of writing skill.* Unpublished dissertation, Cornell University, Ithaca, NY.

Workforce Investment Act of 1998, Pub. L. No. 105–220, § 203, 112 Stat. 1061. (1998).

Worthman, C. (2002). *Just playing the part: Engaging adolescents in drama and literacy.* New York: Teachers College Press.

Author Index

Subject Index